RAGING BULL

HOW TO INVEST IN THE GROWTH STOCKS OF THE 90s

David Alger

BUSINESS ONE IRWIN
Homewood, Illinois 60430

© RICHARD D. IRWIN, INC. 1992

Sponsoring editor: Amy Hollands
Project editor: Jean Lou Hess
Production manager: Diane Palmer
Jacket designer: Renee Klyczek Nordstrom
Compositor: Alexander Typesetting, Inc.
Typeface: 11/13 Times Roman
Printer: Arcata Graphics/Kingsport

Library of Congress Cataloging-in-Publication Data

Alger, David.
    Raging bull: how to invest in the growth stocks of the 90s /
David Alger.
      p.   cm.
    ISBN 1-55623-462-7
    1. Stocks. 2. Investments. I. Title.
    HG4661.A54   1992
    332.63'22—dc20
                               91–24162

Printed in the United States of America

1 2 3 4 5 6 7 8 9 0 AGK 8 7 6 5 4 3 2 1

Dedicated to the three women in my life,
Josie, Cristy, and Rocky
and to my brother, Fred, a great mentor.

PREFACE

Investing in growth stock is once again in fashion after being eclipsed during the late 1980s by so-called value stock investing. The purpose of this book is to show the nonprofessional investor what growth stocks are and make the case for them being the leading stocks for the nineties. Additionally, I will explore some of the areas of the market richest in growth stocks so that an investor can begin his search for great investments for the decade.

As portfolio manager for my company, Fred Alger Management, Inc., I depend on our excellent research department in selecting investments for our clients. Likewise, I have relied very heavily on our analysts. I would especially like to thank Ron Reel, the leader of our medical technology team and Shelton Swei, the leader of our data processing team for their invaluable help in putting this book together. I would also like to thank my secretary, Louise Ulitto, for endlessly typing and retyping the manuscript and especially my wife, Josie, for her inestimable patience while I toiled locked away from my family on weekends and vacations.

It is important for readers to realize that this book contains the names of many companies. These companies produce products or supply services that are illustrative of growth industries in the 90s. This does not imply in any way that at the time the reader reads this book, these are recommended investments. It is possible that they are, but it is equally possible that they are not; the stocks of these companies may have appreciated considerably prior to the book being published and may be significantly overpriced as the reader reads the book. On the other hand, business may have turned sour, technology become obsolete.

These companies should represent departure points for an investor's own examination of the industries that are discussed. A reader may want to consider these companies with an investment professional or may want to get in touch with the companies directly to get an overview of the industries that are of interest. Other techniques that I mention, such as the valuation schemes, may be difficult to implement and may not be effective in all markets, or with all stocks.

I should also state that the stocks I have referred to may in some cases be owned either by the clients of Fred Alger Management, Inc. (including the mutual funds that we manage), Fred Alger Management itself, its parent, and/or one of its subsidiaries. A stock may be owned by me personally—directly or indirectly. Moreover, some of the stocks that might have been so-owned at some point during the writing of the book may have now been sold. Aggressive money managers tend to move in and out of stocks frequently.

I should emphasize that one should never confuse a good company with a good stock; most of the companies I refer to are good companies in the sense that they are participating in some exciting area of the American economy. This does not mean, however, that they are good stocks at all times, or ever.

Lastly, I consistently use the generic "he" for convenience. Half of our analysts are female, so I am well aware that women are as skilled as men at stock market investing. Indeed, my niece, Hilary Alger, one of our top analysts, was an important contributor to this book.

The purpose of the book is not to provide a list of stocks to buy, but to be of help to investors in examining various industries and the trends occurring within them. It would have been impossible to write a book about the growth industries of the 90s without making reference to specific companies. Investors should use the names as suggestions for further investigation either by himself or with a qualified investment professional.

David Alger

TABLE OF CONTENTS

PART 1

TAKING STOCK: WHAT ARE GROWTH STOCKS?

CHAPTER 1

WHAT IS A GROWTH STOCK?

Growth stocks will be the best place in which to invest money in the 1990s. In the 1980s many categories of assets outperformed growth stocks. Among them were: real estate, paintings, exotic cars, ceramics, and baseball cards. Stocks of nongrowth companies also outperformed growth stocks in the period 1985 to 1988.

Growth stocks, after having been investment laggards for five years, have now become very attractive investments, I believe. The decade of the 90s will see them regain center stage in the investment theater. Hard assets such as real estate will not do as well. The collapse of many other categories of hard assets, such as art and other collectibles, has already begun to occur.

A close examination of Table 1–1 is in order. The section entitled ''Annual Compound Growth'' illustrates why one would want to own growth stocks. Column *A* represents an average of aggressive growth-stock mutual funds; over 25 years if compounded at 12½ percent, over 10 years at 15.6 percent, and over 5 years at 16 percent. In any period, this return exceeds inflation. This is, of course, a composite return; it is the return from a wide variety of growth-oriented mutual funds tracked by Weisenberger. Basically, it is what you could have done without thinking; you can do much better if you try and select superior stocks and/or better funds.

I hope that by the time you have finished reading this book, you will be convinced that substantial returns can be generated from owning growth stocks in the 1990s. I will point you in the direction of a number of exciting, emerging trends in various industries that will provide a really good spawning ground for individual investments.

If you examine the stocks in Table 1–1, you will see that aggressive growth stocks, as represented by mutual funds on the whole, while creating good returns, have not performed as well as other stock strategies over the past five years. However, good stock selection within the growth stock sector would nevertheless have generated superlative returns. In Chapter 3

TABLE 1–1
Historical Performance: Weisenberger Mutual Fund Universe

Weisenberger is an organization that tracks the performance of mutual funds. The funds represented in columns *A, B,* and *C* are averages of three different fund types. The computations in column *A* represent mutual funds whose standard goal is investing in aggressive growth stocks. We believe this is a good proxy for growth stocks. Note that during the last five years the growth stock proxy considerably underperformed the Standard & Poor's 500 index. Over 10 years, the poor recent performance also caused growth stocks to underperform slightly. Over 25 years, however, growth stocks outperformed all other forms of investing.

Year	*S&P 500 Adjusted*	*A*	*B*	*C*
	Percent Change in Net Assets per Share with Capital Gain and Dividend Reinvested			
1965	12.8	38.7	24.4	17.9
1966	− 9.5	− 2.0	− 3.8	− 5.9
1967	24.3	66.6	35.7	27.9
1968	11.1	19.7	15.3	14.6
1969	− 8.4	−18.7	−10.8	−12.1
1970	4.4	−16.4	− 6.9	− 0.8
1971	14.4	27.4	20.0	15.1
1972	18.7	11.7	12.8	12.5
1973	−15.0	−29.3	−22.7	−17.9
1974	−26.6	−27.2	−26.6	−21.0
1975	37.3	41.5	32.8	34.1
1976	23.6	31.3	24.0	25.9
1977	− 7.5	9.4	1.4	− 2.7
1978	6.5	17.6	13.7	8.6
1979	18.0	39.8	29.9	22.6
1980	32.4	44.1	35.0	28.3
1981	− 5.0	− 2.8	− 0.5	− 1.9
1982	21.6	28.9	26.5	24.5
1983	22.4	23.0	21.4	20.6
1984	6.2	− 8.6	− 2.3	4.4
1985	32.1	28.9	28.2	28.4
1986	18.6	11.4	13.3	15.6
1987	5.1	0.9	1.6	1.4
1988	16.5	14.0	14.8	15.1
1989	31.6	26.9	25.2	23.5
$100 became	$1,131	$1,918	$1,259	$1,099
Annual Compound Growth				
5 years	20.3%	16.0%	16.2%	16.4%
10 years	17.5	15.6	15.6	15.5
25 years	10.2	12.5	10.7	10.1

A—Growth funds: Aggressive growth (maximum capital gains).
B—Growth funds: Long-term growth, income secondary.
C—Diversified: Growth and income.

Weisenberger Investment Company Service.

I will show that had you bought four specific growth stocks in 1985 you could have made nine times your money by 1989, a 55 percent compound growth rate. Obviously then, good stock selection is the key to making superb returns. Nevertheless, it does help to have the tide going with you—as it will be in the 90s. Moreover, I believe the 1990s will be a period of tremendous overall stock market excitement played out against the backdrop of a comparatively consistent economy.

What is a good definition of growth stocks? A growth stock is the stock of a company that is growing at a rate significantly greater than the economy as a whole is. This growth of the company can be measured in several ways but usually includes growth of earnings per share. Mere earnings-per-share growth is not sufficient, however. The company should be expanding its business and must be reasonably expected to expand for the next five years.

Growth stocks tend to clump together in industries that are exciting and rapidly growing. Identifying these industries is really the first step toward successful investing. With the help of a broker or other investment professional, an individual investor can find the candidates that are the most attractive from within those industries. Later in the book I discuss several industries in which one can expect to see tremendous growth in the next decade.

Investors can also capitalize on growth stock opportunities by investing in a mutual fund that specializes in growth stocks, such as our own Alger Fund. There are many mutual fund groups that have funds specializing in this kind of investment. From the perspective of the individual investor, this prevents worrying about individual stock selection. Of course, it is much more fun to go out and discover growth stocks on your own.

WHY NOT FERRARIS?

Investing in growth stocks or in funds specializing in growth stocks will be a smart move in the 90s. You may ask why should any class of assets (stocks, bonds, etc.) be preferable to any other when it comes to making money? The answer is that there is probably no class of assets that can always be considered the preferred form of investing. All assets have price ranges within which they will trade. Moreover, all assets will change valuation, depending on the circumstances prevalent during a given period of time. However, certain kinds of assets have advantages that others don't.

For example, a vintage Ferrari can give its owner great pleasure. It is fun to drive and beautiful to look at. It also confers a certain amount of prestige. A mansion in Beverly Hills also confers prestige and, in addition, provides extremely agreeable shelter. An Impressionist painting gives aesthetic enjoyment. It, too, confers prestige. All of these assets have one other thing in common, they have all appreciated greatly during the last 10 years.

What then are the advantages conferred by common stock? As we have seen, common stocks do not necessarily appreciate as much as do other assets during all periods of time. Indeed, when the stock market hit 3,000 earlier in 1991 (as measured by the Dow Jones Industrial Average), it was only selling for triple the highest price it attained in the mid-1960s. By contrast, a cooperative apartment in New York City on Park Avenue might, on average, have appreciated by 15 times over the same period, even though prices have come down recently.

Another example of the stunning price rise in hard assets has been in the art market. Sotheby's Art Index, Table 1–2, shows the dramatic increase in the price of different kinds of art works between 1975 and 1990. By contrast, the Dow Jones only rose about 200 percent in the same period (excluding dividends).

This increase in the price of collectibles and real estate came about because of the dramatic increase in inflation following the oil embargo of 1973–74, the globalization of art investing, and the weak dollar of the late eighties. None of these factors are likely to exist in the nineties.

Common stocks have two distinct advantages over other types of assets. The first is liquidity—common stock can almost always be converted into cash almost instantly (near some clearly defined price). The same cannot be said for most other categories of assets. (Try and sell a house in a falling market!)

The second, and most important, advantage is that ownership of a corporation is an investment that *can create its own wealth*. A painting, a classic automobile, and a stamp collection only can appreciate because of the fashion component inherent in their nature. If an artist is popular, the price of his art will appreciate; if he loses his popularity, the price will go down.

A painting itself does not create any wealth. A corporation, by contrast, creates its own value. The fashion component, which is the price/earnings (P/E) multiple, can rise and fall, but the company continues to provide an earnings stream. Thus, the wealth of the company can continue

TABLE 1–2
Sotheby's Art Index ($ basis)

Category	1975	1976	1977	1978	1979	1980	1981	1982	1983	1984	1985	1986	1987	1988	1989	1990
Old master paintings	100	105	131	173	224	255	201	205	239	278	289	303	373	469	754	865
19th-century European paintings	100	99	118	160	215	225	179	184	201	230	249	279	323	421	575	634
Impressionist art	100	107	114	133	175	206	248	267	307	356	380	490	723	1255	1845	1471
Modern paintings	100	105	108	132	178	204	249	245	282	336	364	512	757	1138	1684	1600
Contemporary art	100	105	127	159	197	239	285	342	292	444	497	551	609	856	1627	1456
American paintings	100	129	171	255	315	350	450	450	556	589	667	698	871	958	1371	1174
Continental ceramics	100	121	154	213	261	336	293	266	284	284	284	290	331	467	505	572
Chinese ceramics	100	159	181	241	353	462	445	436	459	486	486	526	581	815	875	997
English silver	100	89	95	124	165	205	175	189	219	261	306	343	381	388	420	453
Continental silver	100	89	92	113	146	179	140	139	156	175	181	201	220	296	367	395
American furniture	100	109	120	134	150	172	209	213	239	289	330	404	459	484	510	510
French & Continental furniture	100	104	121	148	197	232	228	234	257	272	273	299	319	409	500	564
English furniture	100	125	156	195	244	256	279	267	328	382	419	517	634	822	822	867
Aggregate	100	111	128	164	217	253	249	252	286	324	344	403	512	737	1038	983

1. In each case, the figures are shown in absolute terms, without making any allowances for inflation.
2. All figures are expressed in terms of the U.S. dollar.
3. The basis for the series is September 1975 = 100.
4. Up to and including 1980, the figures were calculated yearly only, in September of each year. From 1981, the figures quoted are calculated in December of each year.
5. The Aggregate index is a weighted figure.

to advance despite the valuation attributed to that company. As a consequence, since the fashion component can only be guessed at, it is important to pick companies that are creating an *increasing* stream of value on their own. In other words, buy growth stocks.

Stocks in general, and growth stocks in particular, have a long-term advantage over other asset classes. They can benefit from an upward revaluation (an increase in P/Es); this represents the fashion component. They also create their own value by increasing their earnings. There is also the human component: corporations are managed by individuals who are constantly laboring to improve the value of their enterprises.

As we will discuss later, the amount one should pay for a stock should relate not only to the level of current earnings but also to the prospect of that level improving; in other words, the growth. A growth stock therefore is the stock of a company whose earnings are growing now and, more importantly, will grow in the future. Thus, price of the stock will be much more heavily influenced by the future growth of the company than by its growth in the past. In fact, while past growth is an indicator of the potential for future growth (because it shows astute management, good products, a good position in the market), it does not assure future growth. Consequently, the valuation (P/E) placed on the stock will most logically reflect future, not past, growth.

Investors will almost always pay more for a company whose earnings per share are rising at a rapid rate than they will pay for a company whose earnings per share are flat or declining. This is true even if the company does not pay dividends and may not be in a position to pay dividends for many years to come. Indeed, fast-growing companies frequently make a point of not paying dividends because they are growing so rapidly that they need to use all of the money they make to fuel future growth. This is done by investing in new facilities, expanding their sales force, or accelerating new-product development. The stream of earnings per share, extending into the future, is what shareholders pay for when buying stock. A brief example illustrates why.

Imagine that you have just inherited $1 million and are looking for a place to invest it. A company is shown to you as a possible investment. It has a price tag of $1 million, and net income of $1 million a year. As far as you can tell, its net income number will stay constant for many years. Would you buy it? Of course you would, because your rate of return would be 100 percent, an astronomical rate! (Rate of return equals net income divided by price.)

If the company had a net income of only $100,000, would you buy it then? Probably not. After all, as I am writing this book, one can get a 8⅛ percent return on 30-year government bonds. This return is guaranteed (on the original investment), as is the principal. The corporation is obviously somewhat more risky. The rate of return from buying the company would be only 10 percent ($100,000 divided by $1,000,000), not significantly better than government bonds.

Now, what about a company that will earn only $50,000 (on $1 million) this year but is growing, in terms of its net income, at a 50 percent rate? The first year it would earn $50,000, a 5 percent return, not very attractive. The second year $75,000, a little bit better. The third, it would earn $112,000, slightly above mediocre. The fourth year, it would earn almost $170,000, the fifth year $253,000. The sixth year, almost $400,000. Informed investors will note that the stream of income has to be discounted to present value to accommodate the time value of money. While this is true, it will nevertheless provide a good investment over time. This classic example of a growth stock clearly shows that while a company may appear overvalued, or not very attractive based on current earnings, it can be undervalued and offer investment opportunities if its earnings are growing fast enough.

In the next chapter we will take a much closer look at how to identify and value growth stocks. For saavy investors who are able to identify good growth stocks by looking at earnings and all the other important criteria, growth stocks can offer tremendous investment opportunities.

CHAPTER 2

IDENTIFYING GROWTH STOCKS

There are only two ways to increase revenues: sell more product, or sell the same amount of product at a higher price. Obviously, a combination of these two approaches is also possible. The economy is full of pressures preventing price increases; examples include foreign and domestic competition, direct price controls, and efforts on the part of the government to control inflation indirectly. Consequently, the best way to increase the size of a business is to sell more product.

Unit volume growth is a measure of precisely this: the amount of product (goods, services, or whatever) that a company sells. Looking at unit volume growth, therefore, is a way of determining which companies are most successful at selling more product each year. In other words, unit volume growth is a key indicator to look for when identifying growth stocks.

Unit volume growth is created in one of two ways: by having a product or service that is superior to its competition, or by having a product or a service that fills some need that itself is growing rapidly. Therefore there are several types of growth companies. Ranked in order of market appeal, they are:

Category 1. A company gaining market share in a rapidly growing industry.

Category 2. A company maintaining its market share in a rapidly growing industry.

Category 3. A company gaining market share in a slow-growing industry.

Category 4. A company losing market share in a rapidly growing industry.

By rational analysis, there is a sound economic reason for valuating a rapidly growing company higher than a slower-growing company. Although analytical tools are indispensable to a company's earning power and to the level and probable duration of its growth, psychological factors can profoundly affect market behavior. This can easily be seen in periods of economic euphoria or gloom. Prevailing investor perceptions are then influencing valuations of particular stocks all out of proportion to the underlying analytical indicators. Similarly, investor perceptions play an enormous role in determining a company's prospects for growth—not only the amount of the growth, but its duration as well. And those perceptions about prospects for growth, in turn, help create the valuation that the market gives to a particular stock.

CATEGORIES OF GROWTH COMPANIES

For the reasons above the four categories of growth companies are ranked in terms of market appeal. The most exciting kind of growth from an investor's perspective is open-ended growth: the market for the company's product is so large in relation to the company's size, and the company's product is in such demand, that the company can grow at a high rate for a very long time. Category 1 companies thus tend to provide two layers of growth: the result of a *superior* product in a *growing* industry.

A Category 2 company may not, in fact, be a superior company, but rather a company that is in the right place at the right time. Even though it operates in a rapidly growing industry, the company's product has a certain "me-too" quality—it may be slightly technically inferior, not as well designed, or poorly positioned in relation to its competitors. Once the industry's growth begins to subside, such a company can wither in the face of the increased competition. In short, a Category 2 company is less interesting than a Category 1, although it may grow at a considerable rate for a period and eventually emerge in Category 1.

A Category 3 company is growing because its products are superior; and, indeed, the company itself may be run in a superior way. However, the slow growth of the industry it serves may make this company vulnerable to price competition once the newness of its products or its marketing strategy wears off.

A Category 4 company is one that is losing share of market in a fast-growing industry; it is almost always doomed to extinction sooner or later. It may be exhibiting growth in revenue and earnings—the reason probably being that the industry is growing too quickly for the stronger companies to keep up with demand—but the growth will probably be short-lived. Simply put, the Category 4 company is just not as good as its competitors. As the competitors gain market share, their cost advantage will increase, ultimately driving out the weaker competitor.

Attempting to categorize a growth stock is an important step in making a judgment about its valuation, that is, about its worth. The attempt forces the investor to think not only about the nature of the company's business and the industry within which it operates, but also about the size and duration of any potential for earning growth the company may have. The following case studies of some of the premier growth stocks of the past decade serve to underscore the usefulness of the four categories of growth in assessing a company's worth.

APPLE COMPUTER

Apple Computer is the prototypical growth stock. For the year ended September 30, 1989, it had revenues of $5.2 billion and net income of $454 million—quite a contrast with its 1980 figures of $117 million in revenues and $12 million in net income. The 1980 low for Apple's stock was $11 a share; the 1989 high was $50 a share.

Let's try to imagine how we would have assessed Apple Computer had we been looking at it in 1985.

Apple had been a pioneer in the personal computer industry. By 1985 small computers were just beginning to become popular with the business community. An investor might therefore have envisioned the kind of open-ended market for the product typical of a Category 1 company. For the year ending December 31, 1985, Apple had sales of $1.9 billion. Since 1980, the company's revenues had increased by a factor of almost 20. Financial characteristics were very favorable; indeed, the company was almost completely free of debt. These positive signs notwithstanding, Apple's outlook from the vantage point of 1985 was not altogether rosy.

At the time, Apple faced three major problems. First, International Business Machines (IBM), a much larger and better-capitalized company, had wrenched away from Apple the lead in business-oriented microcomputers. Second, Apple was having management problems; it was in the middle of a transition from unstructured, entrepreneurial-style management appropriate for a small company to the professional management required of a large corporation. And third, the market for home-oriented personal computers appeared to have become saturated, as evidenced by slowing of growth. In short, Apple was beginning to take on the haggard look of a Category 4 company.

Thanks to the clarity of 20/20 hindsight, we now know that it would have been a very smart move to buy Apple stock in 1985. Shares bought at a 1985 low of 7\frac{1}{8}$ could have been sold for 50\frac{3}{8}$ each in 1989. But back in the middle of the last decade, Apple's revenues, unit volume, and earnings all appeared to have reached a plateau. What were the clues, in 1985, that the company's growth rate would reaccelerate, and that sales would double again by the end of the decade?

To begin with, Apple's new product, the Macintosh computer, had characteristics extremely appealing to business, and especially to the then nascent field of desktop publishing. In effect, the Macintosh helped Apple move from a Category 4 to a Category 1 growth company. Further, Apple's management was succeeding in making the change to a style suitable to a large business. As a consequence of these two developments, Apple's unit volume growth was showing signs that it was about to take off again.

COMPAQ COMPUTER CORPORATION

In 1985, COMPAQ was a much smaller company than Apple. Although, like Apple, it made small computers, it had a different product strategy and served a slightly different market. COMPAQ's revenues prior to 1983 were insignificant, but by 1985 they had grown to $504 million. Net income had increased from $3 million in 1983 to $27 million by 1985. Although its growth rate had been extremely rapid, in 1985 COMPAQ was still a medium-size company.

Interestingly, the stock had been less than spectacular during the period 1983-85. Shares bought at the 1983 low of 10\frac{7}{8}$ would have sold at a high of 14\frac{1}{4}$ in 1985—only a modest gain at best. To understand this mediocre stock performance, we need only refer back to the categories of growth. COMPAQ began its existence by producing "clones," computers almost exactly like those produced by IBM. In other words, COMPAQ was at best a Category 2 company, and quite conceivably a Category 4. In 1985 it was assumed that IBM, a much stronger competitor, could crush smaller COMPAQ at will. COMPAQ's sole merit was seen to be its ability to copy its competitor's product quickly. So even though it was competing in a rapidly growing market, COMPAQ was viewed by investors as a "me-too" competitor, and thus was not accorded a very high valuation.

Even back in 1985, however, an astute investor could have seen that COMPAQ was far better than its market valuation. Even though COMPAQ was making computers very similar to IBM's machines—computers that were totally IBM-compatible from the perspective of software functionality—it had become apparent that COMPAQ's producing computers were actually superior to IBM computers in several respects. COMPAQ not following IBM, but rather leading it. This point was underscored in 1986 when COMPAQ introduced the first 80386 personal computer based on the newest and fastest Intel chip, beating IBM to the market by more than six months.

Subsequently, COMPAQ's superior engineering allowed it to be a pioneer in portable microcomputers. These became a rapidly growing subsegment of the personal computer market. Thus, after 1985, COMPAQ became a Category 1 growth company. With its superior products in a rapidly growing industry the company enjoyed extremely rapid unit volume growth. Between 1985 and 1988, COMPAQ's revenues expanded fourfold, and the growth continued unabated through 1989. Although its vulnerability to IBM has never allowed COMPAQ to acquire a truly high valuation, its growth has nevertheless permitted shareholders to profit significantly: shares bought at $5 in 1985 would have sold at a high of $112 in 1989.

It is a popular misconception that most growth stocks are in technology-related fields. Although many are, many others derive their growth from providing a simple yet superior product as a result of cultural shifts, or just from finding different ways of doing prosaic things. The next two companies are good examples.

NIKE

The country's largest producer of athletic footwear, Nike traces its extraordinary growth to a major cultural shift that saw physical fitness emphasized among higher-income groups. This physical-fitness craze included long-distance running, which required an improved form of athletic shoe. Nike was the first company to see and capitalize on this trend.

Nike reported revenues of $946 million in the fiscal year ended May 1985, up from $270 million in 1980. Net income had grown from $13 million in 1980 to $41 million by the end of 1984. However, the company developed problems in 1985 and generated only $10 million in net income.

Even though Nike had the advanced athletic shoe market almost exclusively to itself, it was facing such severe competition from Reebok and others that it had become a Category 4 growth stock. It was still growing, but its shoes were perceived to be inferior, and Nike was losing share.

Nevertheless, after 1985, Nike was able to use its knowledge and technology in the field of athletic footwear to once again offer superior products. Enhanced by an extremely imaginative advertising campaign, Nike was able to reassert its position. Sales started to take off, growing to $1.7 billion in 1989. Net income rebounded to $167 million in 1989. Nike stock, which sold at $6⅝ in 1985, sold for $34 four years later. The difference, once again, proved to be reestablishing unit volume growth. Nike returned to Category 1 status.

FOOD LION, INC.

Food Lion is one of the most interesting of all growth stocks despite the fact that it operates in the rather prosaic supermarket industry. Food Lion's revenues have grown without interruption from a 1979 level of $416 million to a 1989 level of $4.7 billion. Over the same period, net income grew from $13 million to $139 million. And the company's stock, which could have been purchased in 1980 at an adjusted price of $.050, sold in 1989 at a high of $13⅝.

In 1985, Food Lion's stock was selling at $2¼. The company had revenues of $1.8 billion and net income of $48 million. Quite obviously, the company's strategy—of opening smaller-than-normal stores in towns too small to support a full-sized supermarket—was working well. Featuring advertised brand-name groceries in an attractive format, Food Lion was competing effectively against the mom-and-pop stores found in these small towns. The company's unit volume growth, created by opening more stores, was high and its market appeared open-ended. In 1985 the company was located only in several states in the Southeast, so the potential for expansion was substantial.

The example of these four companies highlights the influence that investor perceptions have on prospects for future growth. Apple, COMPAQ, and Nike all experienced periods in the mid-80s when their products were perceived to be inferior to those of their competitors. The companies' stocks sagged during these periods, *even though* their pattern of revenue growth was never seriously interrupted. Diminished investor estimations of the companies' industries, and of the companies' strengths relative to their competitors' led to a downgrading of their growth category. Later, as investors' perceptions of the companies' products improved, and as prospects for expansion into new subsegments of the markets improved, so too did unit volume, and the companies were able to return to a high-growth category.

Investor perceptions of Food Lion, by contrast, remained positive throughout the past decade; consequently, the company enjoyed uninterrupted, rapid growth despite the fact that it was operating in a low-growth industry.

As a subsequent chapter will make clear, growth stocks fell from grace in the late 80s. The value-investing strategies that did hold sway seemed tailor-made to fit the mergers and acquisitions mania that dominated the past decade. But an investor knowledgeable about the characteristics and potential of growth companies could have invested $100,000 in 1985 in an equally weighted portfolio of the four stocks we've just examined and sold them at their 1989 highs for $900,000. Not a bad performance for an investment strategy that had fallen out of favor.

SNIFFING OUT FAKE-GROWTH STOCKS

There is no such thing as a perfect company or a perfect stock market story. Nevertheless, categorizing growth stocks is helpful in determining their value. Equally important is the ability to recognize impostors, of which there are several types.

1. *The Nongrowth Stock.* Occasionally one encounters a company that should have growth stock characteristics but doesn't. Its revenues are rising rapidly, it appears to have good products, and it is in a dynamic industry. Nevertheless, unusual factors exist so that these positive revenue dynamics do not translate into earnings growth.

A good example of this is the semiconductor industry. Semiconductors are being used at a rapidly increasing rate every year; all electronic products, from computers to automobiles require more semiconductor chips with each succeeding model. Consequently, the unit volume growth of most semiconductor companies can be extremely high.

Nevertheless, the global competition in some segments of the semiconductor industry is so intense that there is constant downward pricing pressure. Coupled with the extreme demand made on available cash by research and development, this pricing pressure creates profit problems of an unusual nature. Many semiconductor stocks, consequently, are actually what we refer to as "growth cyclicals"; over time, they have growth in earnings, but they are also subject to wrenching, industry-specific business cycles. This leads to a pattern of earnings that is highly erratic and inconsistent.

So, although many semiconductor companies have many of the characteristics of growth stocks—high unit volume, exciting products, an unlimited market—they have peculiar characteristics that make it hard for any manufacturer to sustain a level of profit growth. Semiconductor companies are one of the few exceptions to the rule about high unit volume growth being an indicator of growth stock status.

2. *Stocks Subject to Life-Cycle Change.* A life-cycle change means that there has been a significant alteration in the fortunes of a company or its industry. This can come from many sources. For example, after the oil embargo of 1973, oil companies underwent a major, structural change because the price of the products they sold quadrupled. This development resulted in significant earnings-per-share growth.

Another example is a company that has had a change of management. Frequently, new management can create wonders at the bottom line by cutting operating costs and trimming overhead. But this appearance of strong earnings-per-share growth, does not necessarily confer growth stock status. Usually, this cost cutting is of limited duration; the market rarely accords such a company a growth stock valuation—because it perceives correctly that the growth can't last very long.

3. *Stocks in a Cyclical Upswing.* Cyclical companies are dependent on the business cycle. When the cycle is expanding, the companies do well. When the cycle is contracting, the companies do poorly. In this category are a number of large, well-known companies. Even when growing, however, they are not growth stocks. From 1981 to 1986 one of the fastest-growing companies in terms of earnings was International Paper. A *Financial World* survey of August 8, 1989, reported that International Paper had compound earnings-per-share growth of 79 percent, ranking it

16th among all corporations. But even with this impressive record, International Paper does not qualify as a growth stock. Most of its earnings growth derived from improved pricing in the paper products market, allowing the company to increase its margins. The lesson to be learned here is that rapid earnings-per-share growth does not, per se, make a growth stock.

4. *The "Wannabe" Growth Stock.* Such stock is offered by a company having the kind of products typically found in growth-stock industries. However, the company cannot translate its products (or the hopes for its products) into any sustainable revenue growth. Energy Conversion Devices, located in Troy, Michigan, serves as an example. The company's founder, Stanford Ovshinksy, is a brilliant pioneer in the area of amorphous materials. From his material science research, he has developed a wide variety of potential products—some of which have had limited commercial success. Although these products have seemingly extraordinary revenue potential in many different industries, this potential has yet to be translated into a serious product revenue stream. Consequently, while the company is very exciting, there is no clear unit volume growth from any of its products, so it cannot be considered a growth stock. Occasionally, "wannabe" companies are referred to as "concept stocks"; they can even sell at very high valuations. However, since many have no earnings, such valuations are sometimes referred to facetiously as "multiples of dreams." Certain biotechnology firms fall into this category, and telling them apart from the real thing can be difficult.

In this chapter we have examined the characteristics of growth stocks from the perspective of unit volume growth and investor perceptions. We have also looked at ways of discriminating bona fide growth stocks from fake ones. Implicit in the discussion has been the task of assessing the worth of the company in question. We now turn our full attention to that task.

CHAPTER 3

THE QUESTION OF VALUATION

The ability to make money in stocks comes from two different skills. First, the analytical—which involves determining the earning power as well as the level and probable duration of the growth of a company. Second, the perceptual—which involves determining how other investors will perceive these facts. The analytical determines the earnings per share in the future (FEPS); the perceptual determines the P/E in the future (FPE). The FEPS times the FPE gives the future stock price (FSP). In other words, the analytical and perceptual factors combine to produce a stock's valuation.

VALUING STOCKS

Valuation means assessing how much a given stock is worth within the context of the stock market or, put another way, valuation means determining whether a stock is cheap or expensive at any given time.

There are many techniques for valuing stocks; some are based on net assets, others on private market value (the value of a company if sold in a private transaction), while others use cash flow. There is no one magic formula—valuation concepts that prove useful in picking winners under some market conditions will fail utterly when different conditions exist. All this having been said, it should be noted that the valuation technique based on what is known as the price-to-earnings (P/E) ratio is the most common, especially where growth stocks are concerned.

The price-to-earnings ratio, also known as the *multiple,* is simply the price of a stock divided by its earnings per share. This measure gives investors an idea of how much they are paying for a company's earning power. Thus, the higher the P/E that investors are willing to pay, the more earnings growth they are expecting. Conversely, the faster the earnings growth, the higher the multiple an investor can typically expect to pay.

There is no such thing as an appropriate multiple. Multiples have varied widely over the years both for individual stocks and for the stock market as a whole. Earlier we saw that there is a correlation between other economic returns, such as the interest rates on bonds and P/E ratios in general. However, this relationship is only an anchor, and ratios can move widely to either side.

The multiple of the entire stock market tends to vary between about 10 times and 20 times earnings. The Dow Jones Industrial Average, which dates back to the beginning of the century, seems to have a median multiple around 13 times earnings. As we have already noted, the multiple exceeded 20 in the summer of 1987, prior to the crash of October. On other occasions, it has dipped below 10. Many factors help determine the market multiple at any point in time. There is the strength of the economy and the level of interest rates (both long and short), as well as investors' general feeling of well-being.

It is normal for growth stocks to sell at some premium multiple to the market; this is because growth stocks have earnings that are growing more rapidly. As a general rule, the multiples of growth stocks range between three times the market multiple when growth stocks are most in favor, and 1.1 times the market multiple when they are out of favor. Presently, growth stock multiples range between 1 and 1.5, a very low level (see Figure 3–1).

It should be clear that it makes absolutely no sense for faster-growing companies to sell at lower multiples than slower-growing companies. Therefore, growth stocks cannot reasonably contract much more relative to the S&P 500 than they did during the decade of the 80s. If I am correct, a reexpansion in relative growth stock multiples is beginning to occur now and will continue throughout the 90s. But before looking at the reasons for my "relative earnings growth" approach to valuation, we need to carefully scrutinize a time-honored investment maxim to see just how helpful it still is.

The old cliché, "buy low, sell high" seems to make eminently good sense on the surface, but it can be very misleading. Many people take it to mean that buying cheap stocks, that is stocks with low P/E ratios, is the way to go.

This approach frequently doesn't work; there are many periods, some of them very lengthy, during which buying low P/E stocks is not a successful investing strategy. A well-known advisory firm began advising clients in the 1950s, using a strict mathematical definition of what was

FIGURE 3–1
What Price High P/E Stocks?

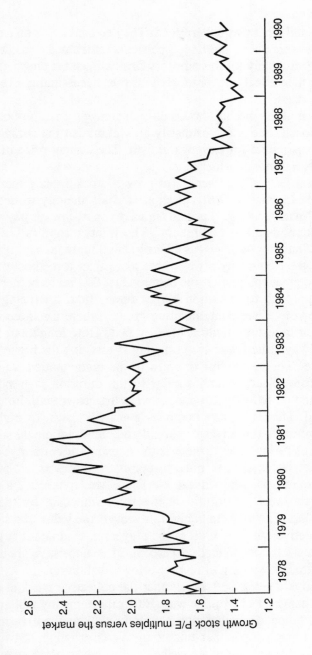

The price-to-earnings ratio of 50 high P/E stocks expressed as a multiple of the S&P 500 P/E shows that even at current high levels, these growth issues have carried more expensive valuations.

Source: Kidder Peabody.

overpriced and what was underpriced. They created a line on a chart, and when ratios were above the line, a particular stock was considered over-priced. Unfortunately for this advisory firm, almost the entire market was above their theoretical line for most of the 60s, necessitating a redefinition of their approach.

In place of the old buy-low, sell-high concept, I am proposing a different approach, one based primarily on seeking out the companies with the greatest potential for earnings growth. The current price of the company is only a minor consideration.

William O'Neill, a successful growth-stock money manager and publisher of *Investor's Daily*, uses a baseball analogy to describe the approach I'm advocating. Baseball teams, he says, always pay a lot more for .300 hitters than for .100 hitters. Who wants a team full of .100 hitters? Or put another way, just as a Ferrari costs more than a Plymouth, so too will a great company always cost more than a mediocre one. Frequently, the great company is the better value, despite its higher multiple.

My approach to valuation hinges upon, first, analyzing and predicting growth. When contemplating growth, there are three important questions an investor should ask: How fast? How long? and How certain? As always, the faster the company is growing the higher multiple it will have. The reason for this lies in the mathematics we have discussed before. Second, and similarly, the duration is important; an investor should always try to predict what the growth will be like in the years ahead. Then, too, as a company's growth slows, its multiple will come down; the astute investor should be able to anticipate such future growth deceleration. Third, there is the question of certainty. Certainty is important because it is not the company that sets valuations for stocks, but, rather, other investors. There are, it is true, a few very large, very powerful institutional investors who can, by themselves, alter the value of a stock. In general, however, the value of a stock is set by the collective wisdom of all of the players in the market at any given point in time. If the collective perception is uncertain about a company's future, the stock will receive a lower valuation.

One buys a stock with hopes that the collective wisdom about the stock will change in a favorable way. Either the company will grow faster and hence command a higher multiple, or more likely it will be more *obvious* to the other people that this company is growing fast and hence deserves a higher valuation. As we have seen, however, there are periods when faster growth simply is not rewarded in the market. During these periods, the slower-growing companies are considered to be almost as interesting as the faster-growing ones. Chapter 4 will demonstrate how this situation came about during the last half of the 80s.

Exceptional periods notwithstanding, I believe that the data I have developed in Table 3–1 is extremely helpful in valuing growth stocks. The table is based on the idea that the stock market as a whole is growing at a certain rate in terms of its earnings. Of course, since none of us can know the future, it is impossible to know what that rate will be. Nevertheless, for these purposes, I have chosen the S&P 400 index. (The S&P 400 is the S&P 500 minus those stocks that are nonindustrial, i.e., banks and utilities. It is a better average to use than the Dow Jones Industrial Average because it has 400 stocks rather than 30; moreover, its earnings growth is a smoother series.) I have taken the 1990 earnings estimate provided by IBES, a service that collects earnings estimates from brokerage firms. (IBES estimates can be considered the Wall Street consensus.) According to the IBES, the S&P is selling at 18.1 times its expected 1991 earnings (as of June 15, 1991).

For a growth rate for the S&P 400, I'm using 6 percent as the long-term growth rate for this index. This has been its trendline rate. (My actual belief is that the decade of the 90s will be one of slower economic growth; conceivably, then 6 percent is too high a rate.) We can therefore create a series of earnings multiples through time, based on today's price for the S&P 400, assuming that the earnings grow at a 6 percent rate.

Moreover, assuming a growth stock is growing faster than the S&P 400's 6 percent, we can determine how high a P/E an investor should pay so that three years from now the multiple of the growth stock and the multiple of the market will be the same.

Table 3–1 gives the highest multiple one can pay in order to accomplish this, given a specific level of growth. Table 3–2 shows the break-even point, in terms of years, for a stock at specific growth and multiple levels. Note the effect of rapid growth. Many people will say that a multiple of 30 is very high. Indeed, it is 1.5 the level of the market. However, a stock with this multiple will break even with the market's multiple in only 1.7 years if its earnings grow at a rate of 50 percent.

No intelligent person would buy a slower-growing company if he could buy a faster-growing one at the same price (multiple). This is where the usefulness of my table comes in: it shows how much more an investor should pay for a given level of growth. The trick is to make correct assumptions about a given company's earnings and its forward-looking

TABLE 3–1
P/E Ratio to Be Reached for Desired Growth

S&P 400 index (spin):	449.6
S&P 400 1991 earnings:	24.72
Estimated earnings growth rate:	6.0
Estimated 1994 earnings:	29.44
S&P 400 1994 multiple:	15.3

	Estimated Earnings Growth Rate																
	2	4	6	8	10	12	14	16	18	20	22	25	30	35	40	45	50
Pay up to this P/E ratio and get 1994 P/E equal to S&P 400 1994 P/E	16.2	17.2	18.2	19.2	20.3	21.5	22.6	23.8	25.1	26.4	27.7	29.8	33.6	37.6	41.9	46.6	51.5

TABLE 3–2
Years to Get to S&P 400 1994 P/E

Current P/E	Estimated Earnings Growth Rate																
	2	4	6	8	10	12	14	16	18	20	22	25	30	35	40	45	50
14	-4.4	-2.2	-1.5	-1.1	-0.9	-0.8	-0.7	-0.6	-0.5	-0.5	-0.4	-0.4	-0.3	-0.3	-0.3	-0.2	-0.2
15	-0.9	-0.5	-0.3	-0.2	-0.2	-0.2	-0.1	-0.1	-0.1	-0.1	-0.1	-0.1	-0.1	-0.1	-0.1	.0	.0
16	2.4	1.2	0.8	0.6	0.5	0.4	0.4	0.3	0.3	0.3	0.2	0.2	0.2	0.2	0.1	0.1	0.1
17	5.4	2.7	1.8	1.4	1.1	0.9	0.8	0.7	0.6	0.6	0.5	0.5	0.4	0.4	0.3	0.3	0.3
18	8.3	4.2	2.8	2.1	1.7	1.5	1.3	1.1	1.0	0.9	0.8	0.7	0.6	0.5	0.5	0.4	0.4
19	11.0	5.6	3.7	2.8	2.3	1.9	1.7	1.5	1.3	1.2	1.1	1.0	0.8	0.7	0.6	0.6	0.5
20	13.6	6.9	4.6	3.5	2.8	2.4	2.1	1.8	1.6	1.5	1.4	1.2	1.0	0.9	0.8	0.7	0.7
21	16.1	8.1	5.5	4.1	3.3	2.8	2.4	2.1	1.9	1.7	1.6	1.4	1.2	1.1	0.9	0.9	0.8
22	18.4	9.3	6.3	4.7	3.8	3.2	2.8	2.5	2.2	2.0	1.8	1.6	1.4	1.2	1.1	1.0	0.9
23	20.7	10.4	7.0	5.3	4.3	3.6	3.1	2.8	2.5	2.2	2.1	1.8	1.6	1.4	1.2	1.1	1.0
24	22.8	11.5	7.8	5.9	4.7	4.0	3.5	3.0	2.7	2.5	2.3	2.0	1.7	1.5	1.3	1.2	1.1
25	24.9	12.6	8.5	6.4	5.2	4.3	3.8	3.3	3.0	2.7	2.5	2.2	1.9	1.6	1.5	1.3	1.2
26	26.9	13.6	9.1	6.9	5.6	4.7	4.1	3.6	3.2	2.9	2.7	2.4	2.0	1.8	1.6	1.4	1.3
27	28.8	14.5	9.8	7.4	6.0	5.0	4.3	3.8	3.4	3.1	2.9	2.6	2.2	1.9	1.7	1.5	1.4
28	30.6	15.5	10.4	7.9	6.4	5.3	4.6	4.1	3.7	3.3	3.0	2.7	2.3	2.0	1.8	1.6	1.5
30	34.1	17.2	11.6	8.8	7.1	6.0	5.2	4.5	4.1	3.7	3.4	3.0	2.6	2.2	2.0	1.8	1.7
32	37.4	18.9	12.7	9.6	7.8	6.5	5.6	5.0	4.5	4.1	3.7	3.3	2.8	2.5	2.2	2.0	1.8
34	40.4	20.4	13.7	10.4	8.4	7.1	6.1	5.4	4.8	4.4	4.0	3.6	3.1	2.7	2.4	2.2	2.0
36	43.3	21.9	14.7	11.1	9.0	7.6	6.5	5.8	5.2	4.7	4.3	3.8	3.3	2.9	2.5	2.3	2.1
38	46.0	23.2	15.6	11.8	9.6	8.0	7.0	6.1	5.5	5.0	4.6	4.1	3.5	3.0	2.7	2.5	2.2
40	48.6	24.6	16.5	12.5	10.1	8.5	7.3	6.5	5.8	5.3	4.8	4.3	3.7	3.2	2.9	2.6	2.4
42	51.1	25.8	17.4	13.1	10.6	8.9	7.7	6.8	6.1	5.5	5.1	4.5	3.9	3.4	3.0	2.7	2.5
44	53.4	27.0	18.2	13.7	11.1	9.3	8.1	7.1	6.4	5.8	5.3	4.7	4.0	3.5	3.1	2.8	2.6
46	55.7	28.1	18.9	14.3	11.6	9.7	8.4	7.4	6.7	6.0	5.5	4.9	4.2	3.7	3.3	3.0	2.7
48	57.8	29.2	19.7	14.9	12.0	10.1	8.7	7.7	6.9	6.3	5.8	5.1	4.4	3.8	3.4	3.1	2.8
50	59.9	30.2	20.4	15.4	12.4	10.5	9.1	8.0	7.2	6.5	6.0	5.3	4.5	4.0	3.5	3.2	2.9

growth rate so that the target company can be correctly positioned in the table. This requires solid fundamental analysis of company's prospects.

An investor can recreate this chart at home in a simple fashion. Get the estimate for the current year for the earnings of the S&P 400—a good stockbroker should have this data. Extrapolate it for five years, using a 6 percent growth rate and create the multiple for each year, using today's price. For example:

	1991	1992	1993	1994	1995
S&P 400 earnings	24.72	26.20	27.77	29.44	31.20
Growth rate (.06)	($25.74 × 1.06)		(27.28 × 1.06)	(28.92 × 1.06)	(30.65 × 1.06)	(growth rate)
Price: multiple (price/earnings, projected)					
$449.6	18.1 ×	17.1 ×	16.1 ×	15.2 ×	14.4 ×

Take the earnings and the growth rate of the target company (say, $1.00 growing at 35 percent) and extrapolate.

1991	1992	1993	1994	1995
$1.00	$1.35	$1.82	$2.45	$3.30
	× 1.35	× 1.35	× 1.35	×1.35

Thus, in three years, the target company will earn $1.82 (theoretically). We believe the market will sell at 16.1 × $1.82 in 1993, so if we apply the same multiple to the earnings of the target company we get $29.30 ($1.82 × 16.1). An investor can therefore expect to pay up to $29.30 for the stock because even if the stock only maintains the market multiple the following year, it will be to at least $37.24 ($2.45 × 15.2) a 27 percent gain versus 6 percent for the market.

This table will not work in every market. The market is capable of great excesses in both directions. Growth will always win out, however, because the faster-growing company will never sell at a discount to the market as a whole for long.

But, remember, as well, that what we are discussing here is *relative performance*. If the whole market drops, growth stocks will drop as well. There is a saying on Wall Street, "You can't eat relative performance."

Still, investors should try to make as much money as possible during rising markets; normally, growth stocks have a bias in investors' favor because of their tendency to do just that.

The stock market should be played like football. When the market is rising an investor should make as much money as possible, just as a football team on offense must score as many points as possible. If a stock's earnings aren't growing and its relative multiple is not rising, then the stock cannot beat the market on offense. A growth stock can beat the market merely by keeping the same relative multiple—because its earnings are growing.

Critics of the approach I am advocating will be quick to suggest that returns from growth stocks should be higher because the investor takes more risk than he might if he bought slower-growing stocks, with lower multiples. It may be true that growth stocks are more volatile than the market as a whole. However, that does not imply greater risk. Volatility is not to be feared; indeed, upside volatility (doing better than the market) is to be cherished. Downside volatility is also to be cherished because it presents wonderful buy points.

So, don't be misled into thinking that big, slow-growing companies are safer. Big companies can have awful results; for example, Chrysler once again is losing lots of money, Pan American is bankrupt, and Union Carbide's earnings are under pressure. Granted, these are cyclical companies, but what about IBM, which reported that its first-quarter 1991 earnings would be much lower than analysts expectations? Observe Eastman Kodak, a company that has chronically disappointed analysts and investors; look also at Kodak's neighbor, Xerox, which has also never been quite on track in the past 10 years. By contrast, Wal-Mart, a great growth stock has overtaken Sears, a classic safe stock, as America's number one retailer.

RECOMMENDED TACTICS

Focus on Long-Term Rate of Return

An investor should concentrate on his rate of return over time. Rate of return can be maximized by investing aggressively in rising markets and even in declining markets. Money is lost most often not because an investor has paid too much (too high a multiple), but because the assumptions on earnings and growth turned out to be incorrect. If an investor pays too much but the growth is as high as expected, earnings will grow so that the investor will be bailed out in time. Retreating to lower-multiple stocks in an attempt to time a market drop is very hard to do successfully, because it implies an ability to pick the top of the market move—an ability which few possess. Also, bull markets are generally longer and more frequent than bear markets, and they have bigger moves in percentage terms. If an investor buys growth stocks successfully, he will outperform the market by a lot on the way up and may only underperform by a little in the down move, while remaining fully invested.

Know When to Sell

The most difficult decision confronting an investor is when to sell. Since most investors are enthusiastic by nature, they find buying easy. However, the sell decision always seems to be hard to make.

Selling should be done for the following reasons in this order: First, if the story has changed, sell immediately. Most money is lost through bad analysis. If a company is supposed to have earnings of $1.00 a share in its first quarter, an increase of 25 percent, and you learn it will only earn $0.80, an increase of zero, sell immediately. This is a material change in the story from what you believed when you bought the stock originally. If a great product isn't selling too well or the new factory is having start-up problems, if the President just ran off to Brazil with his mistress, don't hesitate—sell. You should know what to expect fundamentally from your company; if things change, so, too, must your portfolio.

Second, if your stock persistently does worse than similar stocks in the market or the market itself, sell. This is a warning sign; you may not know the problem, but someone else does. This is not easy; stocks may lag or lead other stocks. You have to watch how it acts. If you have doubts, double your investigative work to make sure there isn't a problem. However persistent, bad action is a bad sign.

Third, sell if the stock has attained your price objectives but be flexible about your objectives. This technique has to be approached carefully. Constantly reassess your objectives against the market climate as a whole—similar stocks and stocks with equivalent growth. Also, just as stocks can have bad results, they can also have unexpectedly good results. Frequently a stock will shoot ahead and appear overpriced; it will then turn out that results are much better than expected and it offers a great opportunity for further gain. Don't be too hasty to sell as long as the fundamentals are strong and the stock is doing well. The ideal stock is a stock like Wal-Mart or ADP were in the 1980s— companies which continued to grow rapidly for a decade, during which time the stock also did extremely well.

Diversify

As I've mentioned before, the main difficulty in valuation is correctly assessing the fundamentals. Professionals are always guessing wrong about companies' earnings; predicting future growth is more of an art than a science in many cases. Companies themselves often can't predict their own earnings. Some don't know until 30 days after the end of a quarter what they earned. If you could bug a corporation's boardroom, you would not only be committing an illegal act, but you would be getting information which was far less than 100 percent valuable.

Given the uncertainty of information, it is very hard for individuals to be accurate most of the time. In order to hedge against sudden fundamental shocks, I strongly recommend diversification. No matter how small a portfolio, it should own at least five stocks. In the $100,000 to $500,000 range, I recommend 10 to 20 stocks. Above $1,000,000, I recommend 20 or more. If an investor is doing his own analysis, it becomes more difficult, but is generally necessary. If something has to give, trade less but stay diversified. The old cliché, "put all your eggs in one basket and watch the basket closely," may have worked for Bernard Baruch (to whom the quote is, I believe, attributed), but that was a long time ago, before computers and lots of professional money managers competing to get the information before the individual investor.

Position Yourself for the Serendipitous Event

In the short term, most major stock market successes are a result of the serendipitous event, earnings much greater than expected, a surprise new product, a takeover. These events are unexpected and by definition cannot be known. However, an investor can position himself to get lucky. Remember the concepts discussed earlier in the book; surprisingly good earnings growth tends to come to companies with high unit volume growth. Most frequently it happens to Category 1 growth companies, companies that are taking share in a rapidly growing industry. An investor can simplify his analysis by concentrating in these types of companies. Remember, the valuation may not be so high if the earnings growth is faster than expected.

Make Sure the Company is Adequately Capitalized

There is currently a substantial amount of discussion as to whether the stocks of small-capitalization companies will outperform the stocks of large-capitalization companies during the next few years. As I am a manager sometimes associated with small cap stocks, most people assume I favor them. Ibbotson and Sinquefield,[1] a research firm, has shown that, over time, small-cap stocks beat large-cap stocks. In the 64-year period December 31, 1925, to December 31, 1989, small-cap stocks had an annual rate of return of 14.1 percent versus 9.1 percent for all common stocks. However, there was a very high standard deviation. More recently, from 1975 to 1983 small-cap stocks were much better performers. For 1983–90, however, they underperformed dramatically.

I believe that the growth rate is the most important ingredient in stock performance. Consequently, I would rather buy a large, fast-growing company than a small, fast-growing company because smaller companies tend to be knocked off track by exogenous factors more easily. However, the law of large numbers is such that there are many more small, fast-growing companies than large ones. I have found that medium-capitalization companies ($500 million to $2 billion) are often the best. They are small enough to have many good years of growth ahead of them, but big enough to have firm control of their own destinies.

---

[1] *Stocks, Bonds, Bills and Inflation*: 1990 Yearbook (Chicago: Ibbotson Associates, Inc., 1990).

CHAPTER 4

THE 90s—GROWTH STOCKS RETURN TO GLORY

Growth stocks make superior investments to other stocks in most periods. In the late 1980s, however, the broad indices, especially the S&P 500, performed better than most growth stocks. Growth stocks' P/E ratios contracted relative to the S&P 500, and growth stock investing became unpopular. The four principal reasons for this were:

1. The trend toward indexation and the institutionalization of the market.
2. The extraordinarily positive fundamentals for large cyclical stocks.
3. The takeover era.
4. The individual investor's retreat from the market in the wake of the crash of 1987.

I will explore each of these reasons in turn. The most important point is that all of these conditions were unique to the late 1980s; these conditions will not recur in the 1990s. In fact, in almost every case, the opposite condition will prevail in the years ahead. Consequently, the 90s will be a great decade for growth stocks.

INSTITUTIONS AND INDEXATION

A substantial change in the nature of the stock market occurred in 1974. It occurred because of the Employee Retirement Income Security Act (ERISA). This act has affected the capital markets ever since its enactment. The bill was enacted because for many years corporations had promised their workers pension funds and had agreed with the workers on specific benefits upon retirement. These plans were known as ''defined benefit plans'' because, after an employee retired, he or she was entitled to a specific amount of money per year.

Many companies funded these plans on a hand-to-mouth basis. When an employee retired, the company simply paid the obligation and deducted that payment as a payroll expense. ERISA clarified the future obligation of pension trust funds. The workers before had no protection in case the corporation went out of business, either through bankruptcy or sale of assets, and was unable to provide the money for future pension funds. Consequently, the legislation provided that each company that had an established pension fund plan must bring the plan's assets to full funding within 40 years so that, actuarily, all obligations could be met.

Some companies already had plans which were nearly fully funded. However, for other companies that were substantially underfunded, it meant having to increase substantially the amount of money in the plan to bring the assets up to a level that could support the future pension obligations. This funding came directly out of operating revenue and, consequently, payroll costs increased dramatically, to the detriment of corporate earnings. It was immediately apparent, however, that a company could compensate by increasing the rate of return on investments in its pension fund. If it increased them significantly, it could avoid paying in more money.

While many pension plans had often previously been managed by the company's bank or even its officers without very much thought to performance, suddenly the issue of pension fund returns was put on the front burner. Pension plans became a major cost center, so by extension the ability to avoid pension costs by superior investment performance made pension plan management, in effect, a profit center. Consequently, corporations sought methods to improve their returns, both in bonds and stocks; they began to hire aggressive, capable money managers who could produce superior returns. An entire industry mushroomed; performance-oriented managers proliferated and a whole consulting industry blossomed. These consultants tracked a manager's performance and advised corporations on which managers they should use. The industry became very competitive.

During the period 1975 through 1980, the industry also became very sophisticated. By the mid-1980s, corporations and their managers were using a wide variety of financial instruments—options, futures, stocks, bonds, and real estate—in an effort to increase the rate of return on their pension funds and reduce pension funding costs. As this pool of assets began to grow, the nature of the stock market changed; money flowing into pension funds became the predominant cash flow in the late 70s and early 80s. As a result, the market became dominated by institutional trading. By the end of 1988, the private pension fund system had grown to $1.1 trillion, of which approximately $500 billion was invested in the stock market (see Table 4–1).

The pension fund world began to change again in the mid 80s. First, many corporations began to close the gap between themselves and fully funded status. At a level of full funding, corporations needed a much lower rate of return and their objectives became more conservative.

Second, in the 1980s a new school of thought emerged, developed loosely from some mathematical work done at several large universities. This school of thought, called Modern Portfolio Theory (MPT), held that the stock market is totally efficient. This means that all information is known and reflected in the market. Therefore, the only way to increase return is to increase risk, which can be computed mathematically and called "beta." An important corollary of MPT is that no manager can outperform the market over an extended period of time. This theory has since been discredited or amended by its adherents, but it was very important in the 80s; it tied in nicely with the confusion caused by the proliferation of investment styles and consultants. MPT formed the basis for "indexation."

The indexation trend developed from the belief that since no manager can outperform the market over any extended period of time, the quest for value-added management was futile. Therefore, it made sense to invest money in an exact replica of the S&P 500. Consequently, a corporate treasurer whose plan was indexed could say confidently to his board of directors that his plan had not fallen behind the S&P 500. Also, costs associated with running this type of fund are substantially lower because there is no need to pay expensive management fees; a simple computer program can replicate the S&P 500 results. These types of funds became known variously as "index funds" or "passive equity investment vehicles." (See Table 4–2.)

Other factors which we will discuss tended to support the S&P 500, so it became more difficult to beat it in the late 80s. This reinforced the idea that the best place to invest was in an index fund.

During the late 1980s, the amount of money invested by pension funds in index funds grew from approximately 10 percent to in excess of

TABLE 4–1
Private Pension Funds (Year-End Outstanding, in billions of dollars)

Year	Total Financial Assets	Percent Change	Other Corp. Equities	Percent Change	% of Total Financial Assets	Credit Market Instruments	Percent Change	% of Total Financial Assets
1975	$ 225.0		$108.0		48.0%	$ 71.2		31.6%
1976	251.9	12.0%	125.5	16.2%	49.8	77.8	9.3%	30.9
1977	271.7	7.9	133.6	1.5	45.5	88.2	13.4	32.5
1978	326.2	20.1	150.3	21.6	46.1	98.7	11.9	30.3
1979	386.1	18.4	175.4	16.7	45.4	120.8	22.4	31.3
1980	469.6	21.6	233.5	27.4	47.6	151.4	25.3	32.2
1981	486.7	3.6	218.5	2.2	44.9	178.6	18.0	36.7
1982	575.8	18.3	261.9	19.9	45.5	204.5	14.5	35.5
1983	682.5	18.5	313.6	19.7	45.9	234.4	14.6	34.3
1984	713.9	4.6	308.7	–1.6	43.2	255.7	9.1	35.8
1985	848.1	18.8	393.3	27.4	46.4	285.0	11.5	33.6
1986	941.8	11.0	456.4	16.0	48.5	305.1	7.1	32.4
1987	1,003.5	6.6	460.0	0.9	45.9	359.8	17.9	35.9
1988	1,139.9	13.6	511.2	11.0	44.8	419.4	16.6	36.8

The third column shows that between 1985 and 1988 the amount of pension assets in equities as a percentage of the total declined only modestly. This was due to appreciation, however, because the net flow in the equities was actually negative as shown on Table 4–2. Please note the dramatic build-up in pension fund assets subsequent to 1975.

Source: Fred Alger Management from data supplied by Federal Reserve Board.

TABLE 4–2
Demand for Passive Equities

Corporate Funds	New Use			WTM Start Using			Total Demand		
	1987	1988	1989	1987	1988	1989	1987	1988	1989
	36%	34%	41%	7%	6%	5%	43%	40%	46%
Over $1 billion	73	71	77	4	4	4	77	75	80
$501–1,000 million	49	49	56	6	7	3	55	56	59
$251–500 million	40	45	44	8	6	2	48	51	46
$101–250 million	30	30	36	9	10	9	39	40	45
$ 50–100 million	25	19	27	8	3	3	33	23	30
Under $50 million	22	18	24	5	5	6	27	23	30

This study shows the increase in the demand for passive equities (index funds) in the years 1987, 1988, and 1989. Earlier studies by the same organization showed the following results: 1982, 10%; 1983, 13%; 1984, 15%; 1985, 21%; 1986, 29%.

40 percent of the total equity money invested (see Table 4–2). One consultant believes that, at present, there is over $170 billion invested in index funds. The New York Stock Exchange believes it is $250 billion. Index funds tend to have self-fulfilling characteristics, as money pours into index funds, it is circulated back into replicas of the S&P. This in turn creates a stream of positive cash flow into the more heavily weighted S&P stocks, forcing them upward. This makes the S&P perform better, causing people to want to put more of their money into index funds.

Not only were index funds taking over a larger share of the market as a percent of the dollars invested by pension funds after 1985, but there was, in addition, a net withdrawal of funds from the stock market by the pension fund system over that period. While the percentage invested in equities remained unchanged over the 5-year period, a great deal of the withdrawal is camouflaged by the appreciation in the stock market. This net withdrawal is shown clearly in Table 4–3, derived from data provided by the Federal Reserve Board. Thus, as index funds were growing, partly due to cash flow, there was an exaggerated withdrawal of money from non-index fund stocks.

Market observers have noted the positive effect on a stock due to its inclusion in the S&P. This is called the "membership effect." The S&P is always changing in its composition and, as stocks get taken over or merge into other companies, other stocks are put in to replace them. When a stock, formerly not in the S&P, is put in, it frequently goes up

TABLE 4–3

Private Pension Funds—Unadjusted Net Flows (seasonally adjusted annual rates, in billions of dollars)

Year	Net ACQ. of Fin. Assets	Percent Change	Other Corp. Equities	Percent Change	% of Net ACQ Fin. Assets	Credit Market Instruments	Percent Change	% of Net ACQ Fin. Assets.
1975	33.1		6.7		29.0%	18.4		79.7
1976	18.9	18.2%	7.7	14.9%	40.7%	9.7	47.3%	51.3
1977	23.1	22.2	4.9	−36.4	21.2	16.2	67.0	70.1
1978	38.7	24.2	2.1	−57.1	7.3	22.8	40.7	79.4
1979	47.6	65.9	13.3	533.3	27.9	22.1	3.1	46.4
1980	51.2	7.6	16.4	23.3	32.0	30.6	38.5	59.8
1981	39.7	−22.5	17.3	5.5	43.6	27.2	−11.1	68.5
1982	57.5	44.8	12.3	−28.9	21.4	25.2	7.4	43.8
1983	59.1	2.8	4.5	−63.4	7.6	29.9	18.7	50.0
1984	42.1	28.8	5.4	20.0	12.8	21.3	−28.8	50.6
1985	39.5	−6.2	9.0	NM	NM	29.3	37.6	74.2
1986	24.4	−38.2	−8.5	NM	NM	20.1	−31.4	82.4
1987	25.0	2.5	22.8	NM	NM	54.7	172.1	218.8
1988	69.1	176.4	10.3	NM	NM	59.6	9.0	96.3

The second column shows the negative flow of money into equities after 1985. This, combined with the increased percentage of money into index funds provided a disproportionate lift for the S&P 500.

Source: Fred Alger Management from data supplied by Federal Reserve Board.

immediately as index-fund managers rebalance their portfolios to include the stock.

Additionally, other instruments were created in the 1980s which exacerbated the trend. The development of stock market options and futures that related to major market indices, such as the S&P, also had a buoyant effect on these forms of investing. Some of the speculation which was, in previous times, reserved for smaller, faster-growing companies, was siphoned off into these highly speculative new instruments. In turn, the futures were arbitraged against the underlying basket of real assets simulating the S&P, which caused an upward bias in the S&P-type stocks. This means that investment firms would buy baskets of S&P stocks and sell futures to investors, pushing up the S&P.

We do not believe that these trends are going to provide as much distortion in the future; therefore, the S&P 500 will be easier to beat. Three reasons can be cited: (1) as growth stocks begin to outperform the S&P, more money will be shifted out of indexation into active forms of investing (active investing means the manager tries to beat the S&P 500 or other index); (2) as indexation approaches 50 percent of pension fund equity investing, we believe it likely that corporations attempting to maintain a balance between active and passive investing will treat both forms more even-handedly; (3) we believe the individual investor, because of the demographics inherent in the economy is going to become (either directly or through mutual funds), a much more significant force in the stock market than he has been in the past five years. Consequently, the balance between the individual and pension funds in the stock market is going to tip back toward the individual and away from indexation.

In summary, while indexation had a significant effect on markets in the late 1980s, we believe that its effect will be muted in the 1990s and the S&P will no longer be as difficult a target to outperform.

THE EXTRAORDINARILY POSITIVE FUNDAMENTALS FOR LARGE CAPITALIZATION CYCLICAL STOCKS IN THE LATE 80s

The Reagan Economic Era began with a fizzle, although the basic concept was extraordinarily positive and radical. The concept differed dramatically from several previous administrations that had essentially favored a greater level of involvement by the government in the lives of private individuals. Correspondingly, this had involved more taxation and a greater level of spending. The premise of the Reagan Revolution, as it became known, was extraordinarily simple; it was partially derived from the conceptual work of a young economist named Arthur Laffer. The Laffer Curve, Laffer's central premise, was said to have been drawn on a table napkin and, like all great ideas, was deceptively simple. The theory held that there are two levels of taxation at which governmental revenue approaches zero. The first is zero, which obviously means that the government will get no taxes whatsoever, irrespective of the state of the economy. The second is 100 percent, at which point the government will get all of the revenues but the economy will cease to function and there will be no revenue to be had.

The shape of the Laffer curve suggests that, as one drives taxes lower, there can be economic growth, creating more rather than less revenue for the government. This philosophy was a cornerstone of the Reagan administration's economic thinking. By extension it held that it was preferable for Americans to retain more of their own wealth, even if this resulted in higher federal deficits; the Reagan political thinkers believed it made more sense for the government to leave money in the pockets of the American people and then borrow it back rather than simply expropriate it through taxation.

Initially, the Reaganites did not believe that massive deficits would ensue. They reasoned that cutting off federal revenue was like reducing a child's allowance, the child would simply spend less. This exact analogy was used, in fact, by President Reagan on several different occasions. Unfortunately, this philosophy may have been naïve. Congress, which was initially half controlled (the House of Representatives) and, in the final years, entirely controlled by Democrats, never really was willing to reduce spending on entitlements sufficiently to offset the loss of revenue from lower taxes and the increased military spending.

The initial years of President Reagan's first term were also affected by another conflicting economic force. Federal Reserve Chairman Paul Volcker provided his own medicine for the very high levels of inflation that had been caused by the excesses of the Carter Administration. In an effort to control inflation, Volcker raised interest rates to an extremely high level. This sent the stock market downward until it reached bottom in the summer of 1982. Another result of very high rates was a mini-recession, which lasted through late 1982 and into 1983. This partially derailed the Laffer curve.

After this recession, however, the economy began a long sustained period of growth. There are several factors that affected corporations during the Reagan years; the principal ones were these:

1. Unemployment dropped from 10 percent to approximately 5 percent. A very substantial number of new jobs were created.

2. There were two corporate tax cuts that occurred in the years 1987 and 1988, reducing the corporate tax rate from 50 percent to ultimately 28 percent in the space of two years.

3. After 1985 the dollar dropped dramatically against other currencies. In February 1985 the dollar could purchase approximately 260 yen and 3.3 German marks. Currently, these numbers are approximately 140 and 1.77, drastically lower.

The three changes mentioned had very positive effects on the profits of American business. The rising employment level created a general economic prosperity that lasted from 1983 to 1990; it absorbed the excess labor created by the bulging baby boom generation. The tax cuts themselves had the effect of increasing both reported earnings and cash flow for big corporations. The drop in the dollar also created an increase in the profits of large cyclical companies.

The change in the dollar increased profitability for several different reasons: (a) it made them more competitive globally and America began to export products that had not been exportable before (such as lumber); (b) at the same time, it reduced the competition from international competitors' products by making them more expensive; (c) it allowed American manufacturers to raise their prices as goods from overseas became more expensive.

This price effect on a number of commodity-like industries was profound; these included copper, chemicals, aluminum, and steel (which was at that time operating under its own import quota). All had big increases in pricing and, as a consequence, higher margins and earnings than had been the case before. Figure 4–1 shows the extremely strong effect on overall year-over-year after-tax corporate profits.

The key point is that during the late 80s, the earnings of large cyclical companies were rising so rapidly that it completely obscured the earnings growth of good growth stocks. It was so common for corporations to have their earnings growing at more than 20 percent (see figures), because of the factors that I have mentioned, that rates of growth

FIGURE 4–1
After-Tax Corporate Profits (year-over-year rate of change)

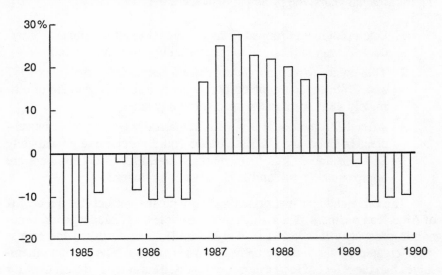

This chart shows the surge in corporate profits in 1987 and 1988. This surge, which occurred for a variety of abnormal reasons, obscured the importance of growth stocks.

Source: *Investor's Daily*, May 25, 1990.

generally considered exceptional were considered rather ho hum for two years. This caused a surge in the valuation of large cyclical stocks. This trend came to a climax in the summer of 1987 when the multiple on the trailing 12-month earnings of the Dow Jones Industrial Average soared to in excess of 20 times. It seemed as though the market believed that these big companies, whose earnings were temporarily growing very rapidly due to a variety of one-time factors, were actually growth stocks.

As Figure 4–2 shows, however, the S&P 500 has a very predictable growth rate; it approximates 6 percent in almost every period. There are, of course, periods where it will deviate for a short term from its trend line, but 6 percent is the rule of thumb for the S&P 500. The S&P 500 is not an index of growth stocks, nor will it ever be! The large companies that represent a great percentage of the S&P are companies whose growth is limited by their very size and maturity. The very lack of competitive acumen

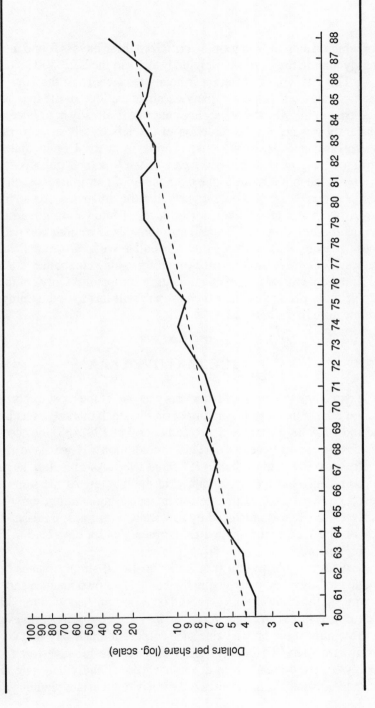

FIGURE 4-2
S&P 400 EARNINGS PER SHARE (actual versus trend line of annualized growth rate of 6%)

for which America is so roundly criticized these days is found most prominently among the heaviest-weighted stocks in the S&P 500.

The 90s will be different in many respects from the 80s. The three factors that made large company earnings explode in the late 80s will be reversed in the 90s: the unemployment rate is already at 6.7 percent and is currently increasing; the direction of taxes is clearly upward rather than downward; and we expect that exports from the United States will be strong during at least the early part of the 90s (and quite possibly very strong in the late 90s due to the opening up of new markets such as Russia and Eastern Europe). This suggests that the dollar may be stable. Moreover, our real rates of interest (the level of interest on government debt minus the inflation rate) is similar to that of our trading competitors. For these reasons it is unlikely that the dollar will fall dramatically in the future. Therefore, investors looking for growing companies are not likely to find them among big, cyclical, mature companies. Only companies that are actually producing their own growth will have good earnings growth momentum in the early 90s.

THE TAKEOVER ERA

The explosion in corporate takeovers was one of the most important trends of the 80s. It had a profound effect on the stock market, especially in the period 1985-88. After the depressed period of 1982–83, the economy and profits began to accelerate. This acceleration, as we have illustrated, really moved into high gear in 1987 and 1988. As a result, a large number of companies became undervalued in the market. At the same time, the leveraged buyout, a technique for financial engineering, emerged in the early 1980s. It was enhanced by low short-term rates, a laissez-faire policy on the part of the Justice Department, and a new class of financial entrepreneurs.

A leveraged buy out (known as an LBO) simply means borrowing money to buy a company, using the company's own balance sheet for collateral. In the early 1980s this could be accomplished with remarkably little (or no) equity. In other words, an investor or groups of investors could borrow almost the entire value of a corporation and buy that corporation from its owners. Originally, this was a vehicle for investors to buy privately owned companies in deals that were friendly and agreed upon in advance, usually with families concerned about estate planning. The concept from the buyers' viewpoint was that the cash flow from the corporation would, over time, retire the very substantial amount of debt put on the company in order to buy it. The first targets of these LBOs were companies with extremely stable cash flow streams (such as soft-drink bottling companies), which had very little debt on their own balance sheets prior to the acquisition, and buyers hoped there were some hidden assets as well. These deals tended to work very well. As the decade progressed, however, the deals became bigger and bigger and soon took on another characteristic; the acquirers began to go after large public companies, in many cases making direct tenders to the shareholders for the stock.

As it wasn't always possible to finance the acquisition of large public companies solely with bank debt, acquirers began to offer a variety of other instruments—such as "junk" (lower quality) bonds. The managements of these target companies entrenched themselves because they realized that they would lose their jobs if the companies were acquired. Consequently, a number of defenses, some legal, some financial, were built against raiders. These included (1) staggered boards of directors, making a complete board change take several years to accomplish, and (2) "poison pills," which permitted management to greatly increase the number of voting shares if threatened by an unfriendly takeover.

One of the most successful raiding techniques was known as "green mail." A particularly nasty raider attempting a takeover would cause the company to voluntarily sell itself out at a higher price to another company (known as a "white knight") or cause management to buy back the raider's shares at a profit. This technique made a number of raiders extremely rich, although rarely resulted in actual acquisitions being consummated by the raiders. It had the collateral effect of increasing stock prices.

As the decade wore on, the defenses against unfriendly takeovers became more sophisticated. As a result, the only kind of unfriendly takeover that remained possible was an all-cash tender at a large premium over the market. A pure cash tender generally *had* to be considered by a board of directors as part of their fiduciary obligation, assuming that the premium was large enough. Occasionally, large premium cash demands were turned down in what became known as the "just say no" defense.

This required raiders to raise substantial amounts of cash because normal LBO lenders, such as banks, insurance companies, and other institutions (e.g., GE Credit) would not provide that much financing. As a consequence, the takeover business would have remained a small but nevertheless lucrative factor in finance had it not been for the emerging boom in publicly traded junk bonds.

During the 1980s, a man who is simultaneously a convicted felon, a billionaire, and probably a financial genius, began to exert a tremendous influence on the financial markets. This man, Michael Milken, developed and then monopolized the buying and selling of bonds that were of less than investment-grade quality: junk bonds. He did this through his firm, Drexel, Burnham, Lambert Inc. The junk bond market became so large and so lucrative to this firm that in his best year, Milken received a *bonus* of $550 million, undoubtedly the highest compensation ever given to an American executive.

By mid-decade, Milken had perceived the potential for junk bonds as a tool to finance very large corporate takeovers. By the late 1980s boards of directors could effectively resist anything but pure cash offers. As a result, junk bonds could no longer be directly offered to shareholders; rather Drexel would offer junk bonds to the public on behalf of the acquirer and the money would, in turn, be used to fund the acquisition on a cash basis.

Milken had such control over the junk bond market that, over a five-year period, he raised billions of dollars to fund a variety of very large acquisitions, some of which proved to be sensible and some of which proved to be vastly overpriced. As a result of this trend, a number of things happened, including making takeover targets the main focus of stock speculation, submerging the importance of good growth stocks.

During this period a group of individuals gained extraordinary personal wealth by using these techniques to acquire vast industrial empires in a short period of time. Some of these empires were extremely short-lived, however. A case in point is the Federated Department Stores acquisition done by Robert Campeau, a man who wanted to become the largest retailer in the world in the space of a couple of years. The vastly overleveraged deal collapsed shortly after it was done, taking the entire chain into bankruptcy, including the venerated New York store, Bloomingdale's. Nevertheless, while the takeover era was in progress, enormous fortunes were made and at the same time a huge number of companies were eliminated from the public stock market. It would not be a distortion to say that the takeover boom rearranged the face of American industry.

One approach to calculating how much equity was eliminated from the market simply takes the retirements less issuance. This method calcu-

TABLE 4–4
**Total Reorganization and Issuance—Completed Transactions, 1985–3rd Qtr.
1988** (dollars in billions)

	3Q 88	1987	1986	1985
Corporate repurchases	$21.9	$ 8.0	$11.0	$26.0
Mergers & Acquisitions	47.9	46.4	46.9	59.6
Divestitures	18.2	22.1	24.4	17.8
Leveraged buyouts	15.4	22.1	20.8	11.5
Total (ex divestitures)	85.2	76.5	78.7	97.1
Common equity issuance	22.8	36.0	48.5	23.8
Net retirements	**$62.4**	**$40.5**	**$30.2**	**$73.3**

This chart illustrates that, using a conventional approach to calculating shrinkage of equities, $206 billion was retired between 1985 and the third quarter of 1988.

Source: Salomon Brothers "The Market Impact of Corporate Reorganization, by Lazlo Birinyi, Jr., A. Pennell Bunn; November 1988.

lates that $206 billion in equities was retired between 1985 and the third quarter of 1988, as illustrated in the Table 4-4. While this method may be flawed because, in some cases, stock was issued rather than cash, and because of other statistical problems, it certainly shows a very substantial change in the nature of the stock market. To put it in context, there are approximately $250 billion presently held in equity mutual funds. Thus, this represents a deletion over a five-year period, of stock equivalent to that which is invested in equity mutual funds.

Many attempts have been made to measure the effect of takeovers on the S&P 500. One analysis done by Lazlo Birinyi of Birinyi Associates (Table 4–4) concluded that a substantial amount of S&P performance was due to takeovers. This does not include the indirect effect, stocks rising because of rumors or speculation of takeovers, which was even more meaningful. When one company was taken over, all similar companies rose in sympathy.

Indeed, the late 1980s gave rise to what one publication has jokingly referred to as the "goofus strategy" (see Figure 4–3). This strategy works as follows: The most obvious targets of acquisitions are those companies that are fully mature, generating substantial cash flow (in other words, "cash cows," the opposite of growth companies); where the managements are weak or inept or both; where the company is top-heavy with administrative costs; or where the company has substantial amounts of

FIGURE 4–3
The Goofus Strategy (When Good Prices Happen to Bad Stocks)

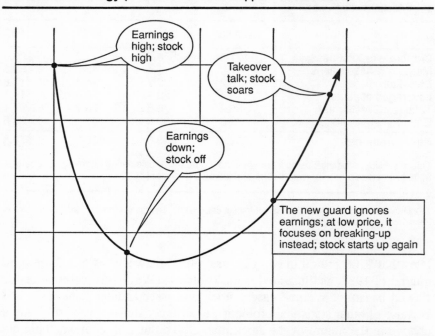

The U-Turn of Value: In 87, Honeywell's stock nears $90 a share in anticipation of strong earnings. Once those earnings don't materialize, traditional investors bail out and the stock slumps. Then—ignoring Honeywell's dismal prospects—the new guard begins talking of a breakup value of $140 a share and the stock goes on the mend. Now, with takeover rumors circulating, the stock is moving up strongly once again.

Honeywell et al.

Goofus buys stocks of lousy companies, does not do his homework, and shoots nine holes every day. Gallant pores over annual reports, stitches together elaborate spreadsheets, grills managements with hard questions, and invests only in the best, earnings-driven companies.

Bet on Goofus to win.

It's a mixed-up world on Wall Street these days: the bad companies go up while the good ones stagnate; and the good-for-nothing stock pickers are handily outperforming the number-crunching enthusiasts.

This new world is proving tricky for many professional money managers, particularly those schooled in the fundamental concepts. To them, a company's value derives from its annual earnings and management. The old guard has its icons (Graham and Dodd, authors of the sober *Security Analysis*), its terminology (earnings per share, price-earnings multiples, return on reinvested capital), and its legions of practitioners (many of whose mutual funds are currently located near the bottom of the latest performance rankings).

The new guard has its code, too: breakup value (the amount a company would bring if its assets were sold off piece by piece—really eye-catching only at triple what the stock's currently fetching), cash flow, and most importantly, rumors. The last begin circulating once bad managements force stock prices down into the range that attract raiders. The new guard's apostles are analyst Robert Raiff, who spins his craft at the investment house of C. J. Lawrence: and journalist Dan Dorfman, who has gunned up more stocks with one mention on CNN than any 200 fundamentalists could if they simultaneously bought the same stock at the market's opening bell. After all, goes the new way of thinking, a raider-friendly stock has nowhere to go but up.

Source: *7 Days*, April 19, 1989.
This is part of an amusing article lampooning takeover-oriented investing.

TABLE 4–5
S&P 500 Percent Gain Attributable to Deal Stocks: 1985–1989

Year	S&P Performance	Percent of Gain Due to Deal Stocks
1989	27.2%	5.7%
1988	12.4	16.5
1987	2.0	13.0
1986	14.6	4.4
1985	26.3	4.7

This chart gives the performance of the S&P 500, excluding dividend income. In the right-hand column, one can see the percentage of gain due to the takeover boom. According to this study, the S&P would actually have declined in 1987 and 1988 were it not for takeovers. Other studies have shown less of an effect. However, most studies show that the impact was substantial.

Source: Birinyi Associates, Inc. "Portfolio Management: The Cost of Trading," March 1990.

hidden assets that are not generating a good return. Under most circumstances, these stocks would be the last that anyone would want to invest in! However, during the takeover era as they had become the most obvious targets for takeovers, they became the most attractive. Deliberately investing in stocks which were selling at relatively low P/Es but were, otherwise utterly undistinguished, was given a fancy name, "value investing." The idea was that one should look for value (i.e., hidden assets), so that one could profit by a takeover or restructuring of the company. Restructuring occurred when management, terrified of a takeover, sold off pieces of their company to make the stock go up.

The paradox was that value investing, which sounds very sage and conservative, was only successful because of the existence of Michael Milken's junk bonds, which were anything but sage and conservative. The strategy worked very well however, and for a two- or three-year period many large companies were gobbled up by raiders, the whole craze culminating in the huge R. J. Reynolds takeover.

In the 1990s, this levitation of the stock prices of mature companies due to takeovers will be much more limited. Funds to finance takeovers have dried up; bank regulations have been tightened in a variety of different ways and will tend to prevent banks from lending to overleveraged LBOs. At the same time, there has been a collapse of the junk bond market and Michael Milken has been convicted of securities fraud. Drexel Burnham, which controlled the junk bond market and was the only firm to be able to place bonds in sufficient numbers to enable the huge takeovers, has gone bankrupt. Without these supports, value investing will lose its relevance. Investors will once again return to companies that are exciting because they are growing and turn their backs on the fully mature companies that are sitting ducks for hunters who no longer have any weapons.

PART 2

GROWTH AREAS OF THE 90s

CHAPTER 5

HEALTH CARE—THE BIGGEST GROWTH MARKET OF THE 90s

In this section, I focus attention on those groups of industries that will contain the largest number of interesting growth stocks in the 90s. This process can be compared to drilling for oil. Most oil exploration occurs in areas where there are known to be geological strata suggesting the potential for large reservoirs. In these promising areas people drill the wildcat wells that result in substantial new reserves. Saudi Arabia and the North slope of Alaska have yielded vast new oil provinces, known colloquially as *elephants*.

In the same spirit, we are going to look at the "geologic areas" of the stock market where the wildcat driller can hope to find stock market oil. The growth industries are similar to the oil "elephants." We will explore the big provinces, examine some of the smaller zones, and finally look at some of the stocks. Investors should not choose any of the stocks that I mention without *considerable additional research* on their part. In the first place, the financial situation with each individual company may have substantially changed by the time the reader has this book in hand. Second, markets are dynamic and both the price of the stocks and the prices of the market may have changed. And, furthermore, an investor should make investments like a portfolio manager does by composing *portfolios* of stocks, not necessarily on each and every stock pick.

Be assured that I make lots of mistakes; an investor who doesn't is either a genius or isn't taking enough risk. Investing should be a bit like batting in baseball. A hitter is considered great if he hits in excess of 330; in other words, if only a third of his at bats result in hits. Similarly, investing in the stock market should result in some hits and some misses. The key is to have the hits be more profitable than the misses are costly, and to have more hits than misses.

Despite this caveat, I am going to mention the companies that have some of the most interesting products in the areas we explore. Many of these stocks may be owned in our clients' portfolios. Some may even be owned by my firm or even by myself personally. Obviously, we want to invest our clients' money in those areas that we feel are going to be the most exciting. However, our ownership of any particular stock does not necessarily ensure that that stock will go up! As a result, I have chosen not to mention the stock symbols, prices, earnings, or financial characteristics of companies. I merely point out the products and how they fit into specific markets.

The most interesting area of growth in the American economy in the 90s will be health care. There are so many subsectors of the health care market that I have decided to break them into several different chapters. Health care in general is not only a very large piece of the economy, but comprises some of the fastest growing industries in the United States. Figure 5-1 chart tells the story: In 1965, U.S. health care spending was $41 billion, or 5.9 percent of GNP. By 1990 estimates for health care rose to $700 billion, or 12.3 percent of GNP. It is projected that by the year 2000, health care will have increased to $2 trillion, or 20 percent of American GNP. This is approximately an 11 percent annual compound rate. This is much faster than GNP as a whole. There are many forecasts for GNP, but we believe that GNP will grow comparatively slowly, $1\frac{1}{2}$ percent to 2 percent per year, with an approximate 3 percent to 4 percent inflation rate. Consequently, nominal GNP (real growth plus inflation) will grow between $4\frac{1}{2}$ percent and 6 percent per year for the decade (Figure 5-1 assumes 6 percent) while the extraordinarily large health care sector will grow at almost twice that rate. It is vast in absolute size as well: the cost of the S&L bailout is presently estimated at $500 billion over its life whereas health care in the United States already consumes $700 billion *per year*. Another measure is that this is in excess of twice the national defense budget.

One of the hidden areas of rapidly rising costs faced by many corporations is post-retirement health care benefits. Many companies, especially those that are or were unionized, promised as part of their pension plans to pay the health care costs of their employees after they reached retirement. If an employee retires at the age of 60 in 1990, potentially that employee will still be alive and collecting health care benefits from the plan by the year 2030. This will become an open-ended responsibility that many corporations will have great difficulty in meeting. As an example, our firm has a client which moved all of its manufacturing overseas. It no longer has any factory employees in the United States; nevertheless, it is

FIGURE 5–1
Rx For Disaster: Health Care's Growing Bite Out of GNP (U.S. health care spending as percent of GNP)

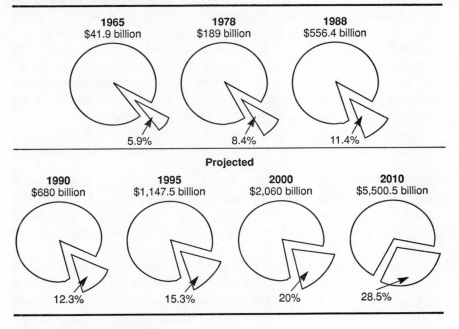

Source: Barron's, June 11, 1990.

responsible until their death for the medical costs of all those who had worked in their American factories. These costs are expanding at a great rate.

There are many reasons why health care costs are rising so rapidly but they are not all obvious. It is not all due to rising life expectancy. In fact, life expectancy is not increasing that dramatically. (In some sectors, such as the black population, there is reason to believe that life expectancy is actually declining). The reasons for rising costs include the litigation premiums put on doctors, the development of new and extremely expensive forms of treatment based on advanced technology, the use of draconian measures to keep the terminally ill alive, and the increased use of physician specialists.

Despite these increases in cost, there will be substantial advances in health care in the 90s. A great deal of funding has gone into finding cures, or improving treatment, for a number of the more difficult diseases that have plagued this country for centuries. There is no doubt that in the 90s there will be substantial inroads made against many forms of cancer, improved treatment for heart attacks, advances made against blood disorders such as anemia and leukopenia, cures for hepatitis, as well as the possibility of a universal hepatitis vaccine. There will also be a variety of new agents approved (by the FDA) for combating diseases that kill many people each year but are not well publicized, such as septic shock. Additionally, there will be new forms of treatment for Alzheimer's, incontinence, and other diseases of the aged. These will be timely, because during the decade there will be a significant aging of the population.

One of the major changes in health care during the decade will be a dramatic attempt to shorten hospital stays. All of the factors in the health care reimbursement industry, including government programs such as Medicaid and Medicare are trying to reduce hospital stays in an effort to control medical costs. There is no question that the tail-end of a hospital stay, which is labor-intensive (nursing staff) adds greatly to the cost of care. Consequently, many types of health care will be shifted to the home and to outpatient facilities.

As we will discuss, one of the breakthroughs in this regard will be new surgical procedures enabling substantial reduction of the number of days in hospital. Moreover, companies are developing other forms of outpatient care. Additionally, there will be many new therapies that will substitute medicine for days spent in the hospital.

These are some of the efforts that will tend to keep the burden of health care costs more controlled than it otherwise would be. You will notice that I haven't mentioned AIDS in my listing of diseases that will be on their way to solution. There probably will be significant advances in the fight against AIDS in the 90s. However, AIDS is a disease that is still spreading in the population and will be a substantial net contributor to health care costs.

Nevertheless, we are on the verge of an explosion of new kinds of treatments for a wide variety of diseases (including AIDS) and, as we enter the next millennium, there will be a greatly reduced number of fatal diseases. Thus, the mortality rate on many diseases that we now think of as highly fatal will be significantly reduced.

There is no question that there will be a great forward leap in the quality of health care in this country by the end of the decade. This forward leap will not be without cost. Thus, people will be cured of many more diseases, but it will be expensive. Consequently, the biggest growth area in the 90s will be health care, and its subcomponents will provide a wealth of stock market opportunities.

The health care industry has an important advantage in providing interesting growth stocks. The advantage that many of the medical technology companies have over their counterparts in other industries—including the data processing or communications industries—is that there are substantial natural barriers to competition. In the data processing or communications industries, which we will discuss later, there are many products that grow rapidly one year but are obsolete the following year. Patents appear to have limited ability to protect products in these rapidly changing environments because patents are extraordinarily easy to design around. Secondly, patents require a long time to obtain. Consequently, the road is often a bumpy one for communications or data-processing-technology companies because they are forced to render their own product lines obsolete at rapid intervals in order to stay ahead of competitors.

There is obviously competition in the medical technology field as well. Nevertheless, there are barriers to entry which do not exist in the areas of electronic technology. First, most medical products have to be submitted to the Food and Drug Administration for approval. This review process, from inception to approval, can take from five to seven years (see Figure 5–2). Second, patents *are* significant in the medical area. Although design-arounds do occur, they are substantially less frequent. Consequently, the combination of a patent and approved status can considerably forestall competitive pressure. Also, the United States has a significant lead in medical technology and dominates the world market for a variety of products. This is not true in technology areas related to data processing or communications—the Japanese and even other countries are intense competitors.

This does not mean that the data processing and communications industries are without their own areas of growth. These will be covered in subsequent chapters. The medical field, however, is one where the application of R&D money can result in a product that has considerable longevity.

Another advantage of medical technology products, especially drugs, is that they have extremely high margins. Under GAAP (generally accepted accounting principles), research and development costs must be expensed as incurred. The net effect is that, after a drug has been developed and has gone through the FDA approval process, which itself is highly costly, the drug has only manufacturing and distribution costs

FIGURE 5–2   Economic Profile of a Typical Blockbuster Drug

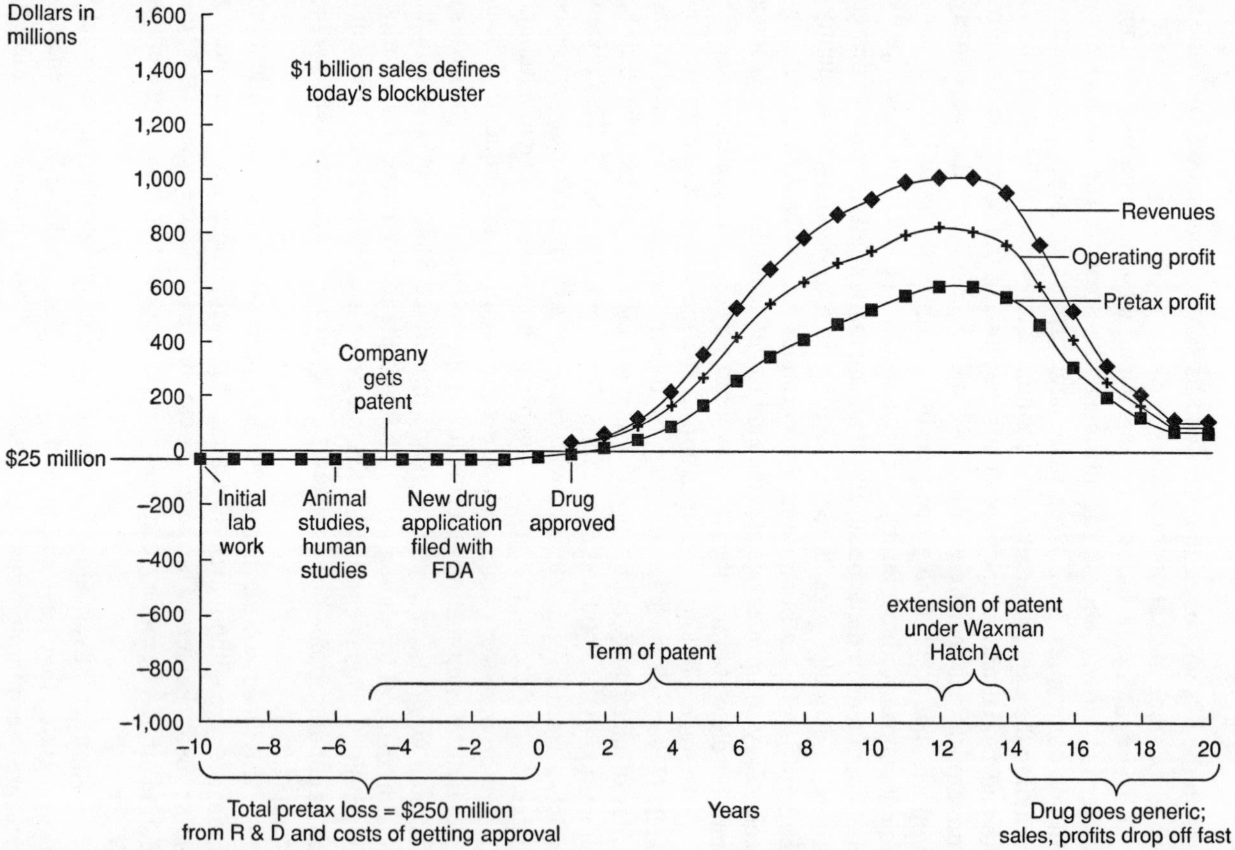

Source: Fred Alger Management, Inc.

associated with it. This can frequently result in operating margins for a given product in excess of 50 percent. For biotechnology products, margins can run as high as 80 percent. Consequently, the return on a "blockbuster" is more than handsome. Of course, it should be noted that most good pharmaceutical or biotechnology companies spend a constantly rising amount on R&D to develop and gain approval for new compounds. As a result, most companies never report an earnings stream of "pure profit," uncorrupted by this large expense category. Nevertheless, the drug industry is extraordinarily profitable for those companies that develop premier compounds.

The following chapters will be devoted to exploring in detail some of the major areas of promise in the health care industry. The area itself is so vast that only a small percentage of the interesting industries will be covered. Nevertheless, we will try to point out some of the potentially most attractive groups and stocks.

CHAPTER 6

BIOTECHNOLOGY

The late 80s is the period when the biotechnology industry became a major business. In 1990 it was estimated that total sales of biotechnology products was about $1.2 billion ($900 million domestic and $300 million foreign), based on 11 approved products. It is estimated that by 1993 there will be 21 new products with total sales of $4 billion to $6 billion. It is expected that total biotechnology sales by the year 2000 will equal $12 billion to $15 billion. In 1989 there were 13 significant biotechnology companies, 15 percent of which were profitable. By 1993, 90 percent will be profitable. From these numbers one can conclude that it is one of the fastest-growing major industries in the United States.

Let me attempt to define biotechnology and explain essentially how it works. Most of what we call biotechnology is based on a process known as "recombinant DNA." Recombinant DNA is sometimes known by an earlier, more descriptive name, "gene splicing." To provide an extremely simplistic layman's explanation, it works as follows: DNA contains the gene sequence for a particular cell material. It is this sequence that gives the organic structure its characteristics. Assume that a scientist identifies a natural organic compound (which is almost always a protein or an enzyme) that can accomplish a certain medical effect within the body. Recombinant DNA permits that compound to be manufactured in large quantities. By snipping and cutting genetic material, a biotechnologist can sometimes also alter the nature of the protein or enzyme and allow it to perform functions that are not the same as those found in nature.

The replication of the compound is performed as follows: First, the genetic matter is grafted onto a host cell. This can be the cell of an animal or microbe; it can even be another human cell. This cell is then put in a growth medium so that the cell reproduces itself rapidly in a natural fashion, creating a vast quantity of the desired protein or enzyme by the process of cell division and multiplication. The desired product is then purified out of the host cell.

A simple example of this is the first genetically engineered commercial product, human insulin. Diabetes, like a large number of other human illnesses, is caused by the inability of the body to create a specific protein, in this case insulin, which is manufactured in the pancreas. Scientists discovered that they could produce insulin in very large quantities by using factories made out of bacteria. They accomplished this by splicing the gene for insulin taken from human cells to plasmids from the cells of a bacterium known as "e. coli." The bacteria was then encouraged to multiply at an extremely rapid rate. The insulin was then purified out of the bacteria, creating a human insulin manufactured in large quantities. This was the first large-scale recombinant DNA product approved by the Food & Drug Administration for human therapeutic use (1982).

Importantly, insulin is a naturally occurring protein and was already given to diabetics in other forms (usually animal insulin). Thus while this was a manufacturing breakthrough, human insulin was not a new compound. The importance of this product was this new methodology for large-scale production.

It was several years before a product was approved for which there was no preexisting widespread use. The first large-scale therapeutic product to be approved was developed by a leader in the field of biotechnology, Genentech. This product, approved in the mid-80s, was known as *human growth hormone*, designed for infantile dwarfism. It was initially developed under a new ruling known as the Orphan Drug Act. The Orphan Drug Act specified that any product that was designed to satisfy a small patient population (under 200,000) would get seven years of exclusivity upon approval by the FDA. This was to ensure that drugs would be developed for small patient populations. This law was compromised to a certain extent when Eli Lilly developed a competitive product and also had it approved by proving that it was actually a different compound. Nevertheless, human growth hormone has been an extraordinarily successful drug. Intended for children who were lacking natural human growth hormone and consequently were undersized, it developed a far larger market than expected (including a black market for use in athletes) and has been extraordinarily effective in treating infantile dwarfism. There is some early data suggesting that the compound actually reverses or retards the aging process. If so, it will be an enormous commercial product in the late 90s. Presently, it has combined sales of about $250 million a year, making it an extremely profitable medical compound.

Parenthetically, let us note it has been proposed that the Orphan Drug Law be modified because some of the more sophisticated "orphan drugs" are being sold at such high prices that, despite the small population base, they qualify as "blockbuster" drugs and are too profitable.

The second important genetically engineered product was the subject of extraordinary hype and a great deal of stock market speculation in the late 80s. The history of the approval process for this drug, as well as its subsequent marketing and the promotion of the stock at the time could be expanded into a case study, if not an entire book. The name of the drug is TPA, which stands for tissue plasminogen activator. This drug is also manufactured by Genentech under the trade name Activase; it is part of a class of products known as *thrombolytics*.

Thrombolytics are a class of agent that dissolves the blood clots that occur in the coronary arteries around the heart. The importance of these agents is that frequently what we generically refer to as "heart attacks" are actually myocardial infarctions. This means that an artery supplying blood to the heart becomes blocked by a blood clot. The heart is then deprived of blood at that location, causing an injury to the heart. Thrombolytics rapidly dissolve the clot, allowing blood flow to return before serious injury is done. One newspaper referred to TPA as "Heart Drano," an unattractive, but nevertheless essentially accurate depiction of the product.

There is no doubt that if this product is administered within four to six hours after onset of the attack, substantial damage to the heart can be avoided and the mortality rate can be reduced. Eventually, this product will be available to paramedics as well as to emergency personnel, creating yet again another improvement in mortality rate.

Several products emerged as competitors to TPA and a wealth of data has been accumulated concerning the effectiveness of each of these products. TPA is unquestionably the most expensive, and depending on which study you read, may or may not have a slight advantage over competitive products. Curiously, the medical community has been slow to adopt thrombolytics, especially in smaller more rural hospitals. It should be noted that the current sales of TPA (about $200 million) are far less than Wall Street estimates expected them to be. However, sales are very substantially greater than for most other drugs, and there is no question that TPA is a financial blockbuster as well as a life saver.

Another important therapeutic product developed by genetic engineering that has a very substantial market was developed by Amgen. The product is called erythropoiten (better known as EPO and sold as Epogen).

It is presently generating sales of more than $350 million annually and is highly profitable. Its primary function is to combat anemia. Anemia is measured by a scale known as a "hematocrit." Depending on the culture and country, a reading of 40 to 50 is considered normal. What this measures is the percentage of blood cells that are red cells—the body's workhorses that carry oxygen to all major organ systems. A hematocrit reading of below 30 is considered extraordinarily serious. The production of red blood cells by the body is stimulated by EPO, which is produced naturally in the kidney.

Currently, there are about 110,000 people in the United States whose kidney function is so impaired (or nonexistent) that they must undergo kidney dialysis three times a week to replace the blood-filtering function of normal kidneys. Not surprisingly, about 75 percent of these patients have hematocrit readings of below 30, as their kidneys are unable to produce EPO.

Consequently, EPO has found an extraordinarily good market among patients undergoing dialysis. Individuals may have other conditions that cause a low hematocrit. Patients on cancer chemotherapy (500,000) and patients undergoing therapy for AIDS (50,000) are two. A potentially enormous market in the United States is represented by the more than 2 million surgical cases each year; anemia caused by operative blood loss is currently treated by costly and risky transfusions.

It is estimated that sales of $1 billion could develop for EPO by the mid-90s as the different indications for the product are approved. It is also an extraordinarily profitable drug. Fortunately for Amgen, they have another product recently approved that looks to be even more important than EPO and may end up being one of the largest-selling genetically engineered products. This product is known as *granulocyte colony stimulating factor*, or G-CSF and is sold as Neupogen.

There are a variety of "colony stimulating factors" under development, including granulocyte macrophage colony stimulating factor (GM-CSF) by Immunex and Genetics Institute/Schering-Plough. Of these products, however, Amgen's G-CSF looks to be the most promising with respect to its effectiveness and also its side-effect profile. These drugs will be used to combat leukopenia, a condition characterized by an abnormally low level of white blood cells. The white blood cells fight infection and boost the body's immune capability.

One of the first markets this product will address is as an adjunct to chemotherapy. Chemotherapy is used in treating a wide variety of cancers. Generally the principle that chemotherapy employs is to attack cells that grow rapidly, which of course include the many forms of cancer. However, such therapy also has the side effect of suppressing other fast-growing cells in the body, including stem cells in the bone marrow that generate white blood cells. (It is this attack on fast-growing cells that causes people who are having chemotherapy to lose their hair, as hair cells are rapidly-growing.)

The problem with this reduction in white blood cell count as an effect of chemotherapy is that the resultant suppression of the body's immune system increases the risk of infections in these patients. These infections are generally treated by expensive antibiotics and may involve prolonged hospital stays. The use of G-CSF reduces the incidence of such infections by 40 percent to 50 percent and has been demonstrated to reduce hospital stays by about the same percent (from roughly 6 days to 3 days). More importantly, it permits oncologists to deliver chemotherapy on schedule without fear of immuno-suppression and thus greatly enhances the effectiveness of the anticancer agents. By reducing hospital stays by 3 days (at roughly $700 per day) the agent may also prove cost-effective and therefore favored by third-party payers (insurers, Medicare, etc.).

In addition to patients on chemotherapy, leukopenia is common to a variety of other conditions (in AIDS patients, burn victims, people with serious infections, etc.), affecting as many as two million people per year in the United States. With an estimated price of more than $1,000 per course of therapy, this product addresses a potential U.S. market of more than $2 billion and an equal amount overseas.

Equally important, the whole spectrum of colony stimulating factors are essentially natural antibiotics. As such, they address, in theory, the worldwide antibiotic market estimated presently at $17 billion in sales. Obviously, it will take several years and a great deal of clinical testing to provide sufficient evidence of safety and effectiveness in these types of treatments, but the potential for these products is clearly enormous.

Another very substantial new product that we expect to be approved in the not too distant future is a monoclonal antibody designed to combat a deadly condition known as gram negative sepsis. A monoclonal antibody is nothing more than a genetically engineered version of a natural human antibody; its function is to attach to foreign substances in the body, neutralize any harmful effects the substance may have, and eliminate it from the system. Genetic engineering has allowed the production of these antibodies in sufficient volume and purity that they can now be used therapeutically.

One such agent, Centoxin, developed by Centocor, and a similar agent developed by Xoma have tremendous potential for treating a gram negative sepsis. There are an estimated 250 to 300 thousand confirmed cases annually in the United States, and more than twice that many who have symptoms (high fever, drop in blood pressure) but who, 48 to 72 hours later, are shown by blood cultures not to have had the disease. *However*, fully one half of those with the disease will develop toxic shock and one half of those suffering such shock will die within a month.

We therefore believe that given the availability of therapy that is safe for the patient and is proven to substantially lower the very high (33 percent) mortality rate, physicians will be inclined to treat all symptomatic patients (500 to 600 thousand a year)—without risking the three-day wait for blood culture confirmation.

This disease is acquired primarily in hospitals as a result of ambient bacteria. Presently it is treated with very powerful antibiotics. Unfortunately, even after the antibiotics kill the bacteria, the bacteria release endotoxins that, in turn, stimulate the body's immune system to release tumor necrosis factor (TNF), setting off a cascade of "autoimmune events" (i.e., the body literally turning against itself) leading to shock, lung and kidney failure, and, often, death.

Though both products have shown effectiveness, Centoxin appears more potent, particularly in those patients where the disease has progressed farthest. Both products have been shown to be remarkably free of serious adverse side effects. With an expected price of $1,500 to $3,000 per course of therapy, these products and others in earlier stages of development could by the mid-90s generate U.S. sales in excess of $1 billion and an equal amount abroad.

Another drug that appears to have great profit potential is already on the market for several small indications. This drug is one of the many forms of Interferon and is known as Alpha Interferon. Alpha Interferon has had a great deal of publicity as a natural antiviral and anticancer agent. Two versions of the product have been developed, one by Biogen, Inc. (marketed by Schering-Plough, known as Intron-A), and one by Genentech (marketed by Hoffmann LaRoche). Presently, it is approved in the United States for only three small indications, but in foreign markets it has been approved for a total of 16 indications, including treatment for chronic hepatitis B and C, for which no treatment is currently available.

Presently, this product is selling at an annual rate of more than $300 million worldwide, with the Biogen/Schering product believed to have slightly greater market share than the Genentech/LaRoche product. With its expected U.S. approval for hepatitis B and C treatment in 1991, and approvals for several other antiviral (including AIDS) and anticancer uses over the next 2 to 3 years, the worldwide market for this product should exceed $700 million to $800 million by the mid-90s.

Biogen would stand to benefit most directly from approvals for Alpha Interferon, as it receives a straight license fee of an estimated 12 to 14 percent from Schering-Plough on sales of the product. At the same time, Biogen, which is a highly creative company, has developed vaccines for hepatitis B and hepatitis C that conceivably might be mandated on a national basis for children. Parenthetically, we can say that combating hepatitis is fertile ground for biotechnology research. A small company called Chiron has developed an extremely effective hepatitis C test.

There is another company to be mentioned that will derive substantial revenues from the biotechnology explosion, although its own products are not in fact genetically engineered. This small company, Enzon, has developed a patented process that substantially enhances the therapeutic value of natural and genetically engineered versions of proteins and enzymes.

One of the problems with some genetically engineered agents is that they have unusually short half-lives (ranging generally from 5 to 30 minutes) and may induce adverse immunogenic reactions, as the body's immune system reacts to what it perceives as foreign substances.

One such product, the enzyme L-Aspariginase, is used to treat acute lymphoblactic leukemia. This disease primarily affects children and is often fatal. The enzyme L-Aspariginase is effective against the disease, but in many cases (up to 70 percent) causes immunogenic reactions, including severe swelling and, occasionally, kidney failure. Due to its short half-life, it has to be given by injection every other day. The enhanced version of this enzyme, using Enzon's Pegnology process, can be administered only once every two weeks and does not trigger immunogenic reactions. This product should be approved by 1992 and, with seven years of market exclusivity under the Orphan Drug Laws, could generate sales of $40 million to $50 million by the mid-90s. This does not seem substantial, but it should be very profitable and Enzon is a very small company.

There are numerous other genetically engineered products whose therapeutic effect could be enhanced with the Pegnology process. These include the CSFs and Alpha interferons, discussed above; the superoxide dismutase (for preventing re-perfusion injury—damage from the rush of blood through the coronary arteries after successful thrombolysis, (discussed above), and natural or genetically engineered hemoglobin, (discussed below).

Another area which will be interesting to watch (although there are presently no publicly traded stocks) is the development of genetically engineered red blood cells. Presently a company called Somatogen (which has recently gone public) is working on a genetically engineered hemoglobin. There is a great need for this product as the U.S. donor blood supply is diminishing due to fear about AIDS, hepatitis, and other blood-borne infections. In fact, most of the blood presently sold in New York actually comes from Bavaria! There is no question that developing a blood substitute, with sufficient oxygen-carrying capacity, is a very difficult task. By Somatogen's own admission, it is a product that represents the most complicated cell ever developed genetically. Nevertheless, during the decade, the need for uninfected blood will greatly increase and the supply of blood, due to donor fears of viral infections, will not keep pace. Presently there are several other companies attempting to develop artificial blood, but, thus far, none of them appear to have sufficient purity and/or oxygen-carrying capability. By the time this book is available, Somatogen probably will be public and should be monitored by investors. I believe that during the course of the decade this product will be brought to the market. Somatogen seems to have, at present, an inside track, although its success is by no means assured.

Recombinant DNA technology will of course be used for other purposes than the strictly medical. One of the companies we have looked at is using genetic engineering to develop "designer" vegetables, that is, absolutely perfect, beautiful carrots, etc. Whether this approach is successful (or desired) remains to be seen. Nevertheless, we expect this decade to show a proliferation of genetically engineered vegetables, fruits, animal vaccines, and a wide variety of diagnostic tests. Presently several of the diagnostic tests that have come onto the market (including those sold over-the-counter such as the do-it-at-home pregnancy tests) are based on recombinant DNA. These developments merit watching.

Products that will be developed in the future, in addition to those I have mentioned, include all of the interferon family, beta and gamma,

Factor 8 for leukemia, and some promising agents for AIDS. There is no question that there will be many additional products. There will be extraordinarily fertile ground to invest in during the decade.

Many biotechnology stocks, including the ones we discussed, have partially discounted the profits from the products that we see coming in the future; as stocks they are certainly not undiscovered. Consequently, they have large market capitalizations in relation to their current profitability. They are also very volatile. Therefore they must be approached with caution and significant analysis. Nevertheless, health care will be one of America's fastest-growing industries and a great deal of money will be made in the area over the course of the 90s.

KEY INVESTMENT POINTS

1. The biotechnology industry (also called simply "Biotech") will be one of America's fastest-growing industries during the decade. A number of stocks will be excellent investments.

2. The companies in this industry can be divided into two groups, those with approved products, sales and earnings (such as Amgen) and those that are working on getting products approved. The first group can be valued on a multiple of its earnings, the second on the expectation of what the products might earn once approved. Both types are very volatile, the second especially so. They are not for the faint of heart or weak of stomach.

3. Biotech companies can labor many years to get only one product approved and on the market. However, one product alone can generate hundreds of millions of dollars in revenues with gross margins of 80 percent or better. This is why there is so much speculation in these stocks, and valuations get so high for companies that don't earn money.

4. Once a product is approved, it is sheltered from competition by patents, the FDA, and the difficulty of designing and producing these agents. This makes a successful company less vulnerable than companies in other businesses.

5. When a company gets a product approved its stock can be a rocket like Amgen's after the EPO and G-CSF approvals or plunge like a rock like Genentech's after the TPA approval—depending on

how well the drugs do versus expectations. An investor should know what the "street" expects. Usually, however, product approvals make stocks rise substantially.

6. During the course of every year Biotech stocks go through at least one hot period and one cold period. During the cold period, stocks with no approved products can drop significantly. During hot periods, they can attain very lofty valuations. An investor should watch a few key stocks to see if the group is doing well or not; they tend to move together.

7. A Biotech investor can spend a great deal of time worrying about FDA approval for his company's product. My experience is that there is little logic to the FDA process and it always takes longer than anticipated. As a stock gets closer to approval, it can rise and fall frequently as investors get alternately excited and discouraged.

8. A high degree of specialized knowledge is required to track these stocks. As it has been a hot group there are numerous brokerage firms with expertise. Seek one with a good Biotech analyst. Another good approach is to buy a good sector fund, specializing in this industry. This will ensure good diversification and coverage by managers with full-time expertise.

CHAPTER 7

CONVENTIONAL DRUG COMPANIES

While biotechnology will be one of the fastest growing areas of health care over the next 10 years, several larger, traditional pharmaceutical companies will also experience significant growth. Indeed, the pharmaceutical industry is one of few industries where very large companies will experience excellent growth in the 90s. This will occur for several reasons. First, as we have discussed, the amount of money being directed toward health care is going to increase dramatically during the decade. Second, following the enactment of the Waxman-Hatch amendments in 1984, which effectively shortened the commercial product lives of existing drugs, there began an acceleration in new drug discovery and development spending at all major pharmaceutical companies. Adding the typical 7- to 10-year development cycle to that 1984 base year would imply a wave of new-product introductions in the 1991 to 1994 period, and that is precisely what is occurring. Third, because of patent protection, the competition is less intense than it is in many industries. Fourth, many of the large pharmaceutical companies are extremely well managed; they have strong, well-entrenched distribution capability, and unlike many other industries, limited foreign competition. Also, the demand for their products is already well established (the diseases exist).

There are several drugs that should come on the market in the 90s (or were approved in the late 80s and will be ramping-up in the 90s) that will cause substantial upward earnings-per-share increases for their producers, despite the very large capitalization of the companies that created them. I will discuss the major companies that have exciting products, because they could all be excellent stocks for the 90s.

Merck is one of the largest companies in the United States as measured by market value. Nevertheless, Merck has frequently been called one of the best, if not the best, managed American company. The company has an almost extraordinarily productive R&D capability, which seems to develop one blockbuster drug after another. At the same time, it also has excellent distribution capability. Its detail force (which is what the drug industry calls a sales force) is among the best. It is our expectation that Merck will maintain at least a 15 percent earnings growth rate for much of the 90s. In the early years, that growth rate could be higher. This rate will be near the top for very big companies.

One of the principal reasons why this growth rate could be higher is a drug called Mevacor and another sister drug called Zocor. These drugs, which were approved in 1987, address the major cause of death in the United States today, coronary heart disease (CHD), or atherosclerosis—the clogging of the coronary arteries (which supply blood to the heart) by buildup of atherosclerotic plaque resulting from excessive levels of blood cholesterol. It has been clinically proven that for people with cholesterol counts in excess of 250 milliliters per deciliter of blood, each 1 percent reduction in the cholesterol count reduces their chances for dying from CHD (principally heart attack) by 2 percent. Only recently, however, have truly safe and effective agents been available for achieving these results. Merck's Mevacor and Zocor, the first of these products on the market, should produce combined sales of close to $1 billion in 1990, after only three years of marketing.

A similar agent, Pravachol from Bristol-Meyers Squibb, should be introduced in the United States in 1991. The potential market for this class of products is very large. In the United States alone, more than 20 million people are potential candidates for drug therapy, based on cholesterol counts in excess of 250. We believe many, if not most of these people will eventually receive chronic drug therapy for this ailment. At about $1.50 per day, the manufacturer of these products receives over $500 per year of revenue for each patient. With 20 million potential patients in the United States, less than 2 million of whom are currently on drug therapy, the potential market is vast (i.e., $10 billion in the United States and a like amount overseas).

Merck also has in its pipeline another exciting drug, Proscar. This drug is in late Phase 3 clinicals and we expect it will be filed for U.S. approval in early 1991. This drug is intended for benign prostatic hypertrophy, or swelling of the prostrate gland; this affects 50 percent of all men over the age of 50, and 80 percent of all men over the age of 80. Essentially, the result of this disease is that the enlarged prostate inhibits, or in some cases, actually prevents urination, and is accompanied by severe discomfort and pain. Presently, it is treated in severe cases (about 450,000 a year) by removing the prostate in a distinctly uncomfortable and expensive operation. These operations cost, in aggregate, well over $1 billion a year. However, only a small percentage of patients are treated, as there are an estimated 5 to 10 million men presently suffering from this ailment in some form. We expect that a great many of these individuals will be treated with Proscar and that, due to its cost advantage compared to surgery, it can be priced fairly high (i.e., about $1.50 per day, or $500 per year). If about one-third or 3 million patients, are treated, this would represent a $1.5 billion U.S. market. The foreign potential should be roughly equivalent.

Another interesting new Merck product is alendronate (this is the generic name for the product; it has not yet been given a trade name). This is for the treatment of osteoporosis. Osteoporosis is a disease which affects postmenopausal women, causing bones to become extremely brittle. Some believe it is one of the major reasons for high medical and hospital costs for the elderly because of the frequent incidence of hip fractures. It will, therefore, most likely be a money-saving product overall. The patient pool is estimated at more than 20 million people in the United States and a like amount abroad. We expect alendronate to be on the market in the mid-90s. It was recently announced that Procter & Gamble is working on a similar drug; Merck's product, however, is a second-generation drug and may prove more effective. Merck is already a substantial company, but based on its pipeline of new drugs, including those mentioned above and others expected in the late 90s, it more than meets our criteria as a premier growth company.

Another large pharmaceutical company that appears to have several promising drugs is Eli Lilly & Co. Lilly has a wonderful product Prozac, which already has surged to annual revenues of over $750 million since approval in May of 1988. We expect, however, that this drug will continue to grow and gain new indications throughout the early part of the 90s.

Prozac is, without any question, the most effective chemical treatment for depression, and lacks most of the troublesome side effects common to other antidepressants. We believe that this product could generate revenues over $1.5 billion by the mid-90s for its depression indication alone. Moreover, it appears that Prozac has the potential to get several new very lucrative indications. The first is for controlling obesity. Obesity is medically defined as being 20 percent over the target weight for one's height and sex. There are 34 million people in the United States who are considered clinically obese, 60 million worldwide. Hovan (Prozac's name for this indication) is unusually effective in causing weight loss and it is one of the few drugs that is effective without being addictive at the same time (as amphetamines were). Losing weight on Hovan is a slow, but persistent process. The recommended regimen costs $150 a month, and is recommended for five months. It causes a weight loss of a consistent five to six pounds a month. While the weight loss is not substantial in any month, it cumulates.

Hovan works by dampening compulsive behavior such as overeating. It may be an effective agent for drug abuse, alcoholism, and smoking. It is of a class of agents known as serotonin uptake inhibitors that work by increasing the availability in the brain of the neurotransmitter serotonin, whose absence is associated with depression, bulemia, and other compulsive disorders.

Another potentially very lucrative product for Lilly is a drug called Quinelorane which is in Phase 3 clinical trials. We expect it to be approved in the mid-90s. Quinelorane is indicated for the treatment of sexual dysfunction (i.e., for enhancing libido) in both men and women. There are 10 million men, in the United States alone, suffering from this particular ailment. While this drug may have some troublesome side effects (e.g., nausea, for which no further explanation is needed), if it can overcome these through dosing changes or chemical manipulation, it has enormous potential, as no effective therapy for this problem now exists.

Bristol-Meyers Squibb (BMY) is also entering a very positive period in its new-drug development. Not only does it have the substantial potential of Pravachol (refer to earlier section on Merck) to look forward to in the 90s, it also has a drug in test called Videx that appears to be the most interesting and effective treatment for AIDS. Videx will be a follow-on for AZT. While it is too early to speculate on the market size and the effectiveness of Videx, it does have a substantial potential, at least equivalent to that of AZT, which generates about $400 million in annual revenues.

BMY also dominates the market for cancer chemotherapy, selling over 20 different anti-cancer agents that represent about $80 million in annual sales and a 20 percent worldwide market share (40 percent in the United States). This class of agents is growing at a 15 percent to 20 percent rate currently and stands to match or possibly exceed that rate in the future, as the launch of the various colony-stimulating factors (see Chapter 6 on biotechnology) and Glaxo's Zofran (see below) make standard cancer chemotherapy more tolerable, safer, and more effective. Finally, the company's Buspar antianxiety agent, the first such agent that does not have addictive properties (as does Valium), should grow steadily after a slow start (it was hindered by the lack of an initial euphoric effect that patients had become accustomed to in older tranquilizers).

Glaxo should be mentioned because, even though it is a British company, its stock does trade in the United States and it has two potentially very lucrative products that will most likely be approved in the 90s. The first product, Zofran, will not only be a big product for Glaxo, but should greatly enhance BMY's chemotherapy product line. Zofran is an antiemetic that significantly reduces the amount of vomiting in patients who are undergoing chemotherapy. A chemotherapy patient may have vomiting or retching episodes 13 to 14 times a day. Zofran reduces this to three to four times a day on average. The importance of this product and other products, such as Amgen's G-CSF (see Chapter 6), is that they will permit accelerated chemotherapy treatment. This, in turn, will improve the treatment for many forms of cancer. In fact, it has been discovered that many doctors often prescribe chemotherapy doses substantially below the optimal because the patient cannot tolerate full dosages.

Imitrex is another potential blockbuster that Glaxo has submitted to the FDA for approval. This drug is used to help control migraine headaches. It is estimated that there are at least 10 million Americans, and perhaps twice that many non–Americans, who suffer anywhere from 3 (moderate) to 50 (high) migraine attacks per year. Currently, no consistently effective therapy exists for those excruciatingly painful and debilitating attacks. Imitrex was developed specifically by Glaxo to address what is now believed to be a major cause of migraines: low levels of the neurotransmitter 5-HT1. That condition allows the swelling of intracranial blood vessels that then press against sensitive pain receptors in the head and neck. Approval for this product should come in the 1993–95 period, and if the clinical results made public to date are validated by regulatory scrutiny, the product could have extremely large revenues.

The next company to note is Schering-Plough. Schering has several drugs that look like they have excellent potential. Their colony-stimulating factor, a GM-CSF (see Chapter 6 on biotechnology for G-CSF discussion) trade-named Leumax, should be approved in 1991. Currently, we do not believe that Schering's product is quite as good as Amgen's. However, given Schering's proven marketing capability and the virtually untapped market for this kind of therapy, Schering should take a meaningful share of what could be a $2 billion plus market by the mid-90s.

Another of their important drugs is Claritin—a nonsedating antihistamine. There are two which are already on the market; however, Claritin has the advantage of a once-a-day regimen and an extremely short onset of action. We expect this drug to generate sales of at least $400 million by the mid-90s, with U.S. approval expected in 1991.

Finally, Schering has two potentially major drugs already on the market but in early stages of commercial development. Foremost is Intron-A, licensed from Biogen (and discussed in the chapter on Biotechnology). It should move from this year's estimated $150 million in sales to perhaps $500 million in the mid-90s because of several new indications (particularly for hepatitis B and C). Another is Eulexin, an agent for prostate cancer, which should move from about $70 million this year, mostly foreign, to perhaps $300 million by 1995, as the clinical data supporting its wider use are developed.

Another major drug company which appears particularly well-positioned for acceleration in growth in the 1990s is Pfizer. After five years of sluggish earnings growth, occasioned by the maturation of key products and a rapid acceleration in research spending and sales force expansion, the company appears poised for rapid growth as its investments begin to pay off. Specifically, the company has nine new pharmaceutical products either recently approved, filed with regulatory agencies, or in late stages of development, including at least three potential $1 billion agents: (1) Procardia XL, an off-patent agent for angina and hypertension combined with Alza's Oros delivery system (see discussion on Alza below and in Chapter 8); (2) Diflucan, an anti-fungal agent, in both injectable and oral form, addressing a major potential market of immunocompromised patients (AIDS sufferers, chemotherapy patients, etc.) in which neither their own immune systems or older anti-fungal agents have proven effective in combating serious fungal infections; and (3) Sertraline, a Prozac-like antidepressant with potentially a somewhat better safety profile.

Lastly, there is a small drug maker which has two potentially interesting drugs. This company, Forest Laboratories, currently sells mostly branded generics. These are off-patent drugs too small to attract major generic competition but which have therapeutic utility and are marketed by Forest's detail force to physicians as though they are regular patented products. Forest's two original drugs that are under development look promising. One is a drug called Micturin, which is a product for urinary incontinence. There are two kinds of incontinence, urge incontinence and stress incontinence. Urge incontinence results from an inability to control the muscles surrounding the bladder and may have a U.S. patient population of as many as 5 million, mostly older people. We estimate that this drug could be a $100 million product, which would be substantial for a company of Forest's size ($170 million in sales). Forest's second product, Synapton, is showing early signs of being an effective treatment for Alzheimer's disease. Needless to say, any cure for Alzheimer's disease would be extremely lucrative, as an estimated 6 million Americans suffer from it and there is no cure.

Generally, the growth of the health care industry should be directly beneficial to the large pharmaceutical companies. As mentioned, there are an unprecedented number of new drugs that will be released onto the market, which should by the end of the decade greatly improve the level of health care in this country. Many diseases that formerly had no hope of cure will now be attacked effectively. This should be good for the quality of life in this country, and even the very large companies we discussed should offer significant growth stocks in the 90s.

KEY INVESTMENT POINTS

1. Conventional drug companies could continue to grow much faster during the 90s (12–20 percent) than the average American company, despite their large size in revenues and market capitalization.

2. American drug companies are protected against competition by the FDA and patents and are strong competitors against most foreign companies.

3. New products frequently command premium prices because of the inelasticity of health care. Small therapeutic advances generate big price premiums.

4. Gross margins on drugs are very high. However, drug companies are dependent on a high level of research and development spending to generate subsequent growth.

5. An investor should be aware of a company's current products and also the timing of approvals of future products. Even in large drug companies one or two blockbuster drugs can alter the future growth rate significantly.

6. Drug companies derive much of their revenues from foreign sales. A strong dollar can sometimes weaken earnings.

CHAPTER 8

NEW MEDICAL TECHNOLOGIES

Not all useful and lucrative medical products are drugs. There is a substantial amount of new medical technology that is going to provide a significant improvement in patient care over the next 10 years.

Although these technological breakthroughs are frequently accompanied by an overall reduction in treatment costs that is not always the case. Medical technology has the characteristic that, unlike data processing technology, a small improvement in the quality of the product frequently results in a large increase in the price. Also, new technologies tend to be priced very aggressively.

As we have noted, medical products are relatively price inelastic. Sick people want to get well in the most effective way and are often willing to incur a higher level of expense. Also, this high level of expense is usually borne by third party payers such as insurance or Medicare. Of course the cost of medical insurance is rising rapidly; in some years the increase is huge. Frequently, however, the cost of medical insurance is borne by corporate entities rather than individuals, removing any sense of advancing medical costs.

Because of the possibility for aggressive pricing, new medical devices are frequently much more profitable over time than data processing devices. This creates good corporate earnings growth and substantial stock performance.

Probably one of the most important advances in medical technology is currently being made in the field of surgery. Here, new technology is making giant leaps forward in terms of effectiveness and of cost reduction, because surgery is becoming far less invasive, and consequently requires shorter hospital stays.

One company in particular seems to be in the lead of this trend, U.S. Surgical, the company that developed the market for staples as a replacement for sutures. Over the years the company developed a wide variety of instruments that are capable of laying down a series of staples in a large number of surgical situations. These staples are superior to sutures in many applications because they can be put in quickly with less trauma to the patient, they require less technical skill, and frequently can be put in difficult places. The surgical staple market has grown dramatically over the last 10 years, rising to $350 million in this country. U.S. Surgical has 70 percent of the market. Additionally, $170 million worth are sold overseas and U.S. Surgical has an 85 percent to 90 percent share of that market. Usage of staples also continues to grow much more rapidly than the use of sutures.

The development of this market put U.S. Surgical in a unique position; the company became a resource for training surgeons in a wide variety of medical specialties. Staples are used in a large number of operations, and as a result, doctors have been exposed to buying equipment from this company and to using the company as a training resource.

The growth of U.S. Surgical could be quite dramatic over the next decade. The key to this growth is a variety of new instruments that facilitate less-invasive abdominal surgery. These new forms of surgery really took hold in the 80s with the development of arthroscopic surgery on knees, a technique far less invasive than conventional knee surgery that allows patients to get back on their feet much sooner than did the older methods. A variety of other new instruments were developed in the 80s, including a number of endoscopes for seeing images inside the body and a variety of new laser tools that have the ability to cut and cauterize with remarkable precision.

The most dramatic new advance in surgery has been a kit developed by U.S. Surgical (which is working in conjunction with Medical Care International, a company which we will discuss in Chapter 8). This kit allows surgeons to perform an operation that goes by the difficult name of laparoscopic cholecystectomy, a new technique for removing gall bladders. There are 500,000 gall bladder operations annually in this country, a substantial market.

Traditionally, a gall bladder removal is performed as follows: the abdomen is sliced wide open and the gall bladder removed by conventional surgery that involves cutting through layers of muscle. The new technique is different: a thin trocar (a small funnel) is inserted into the abdomen through the navel. The surgeon then inserts a laser tool through the trocar with which to cut off the gall bladder and cauterize the wound, simultaneously. The gall bladder is withdrawn through the trocar. The advantages of this technique are extraordinary. First, the surgery can be performed on an outpatient basis as opposed to a four- to five-day hospital stay for conventional surgery. While the operation takes slightly longer (90 minutes versus 65 minutes), the recuperative period is vastly shorter, five days as opposed to four weeks. Also, the scar is a half inch versus nine inches in conventional surgery. The loss of blood is a half teaspoon versus several pints. More importantly, from the patient's perspective, the cost of the surgery is reduced, on average, by over $1,500, despite the fact that the surgeon himself makes more money (by $400 to $500). This form of surgery is definitely a "win, win" situation. Presently, there are now 20,000 surgeons trained in this procedure out of the 34,000 general surgeons. However, this is much larger than even one year ago, so the market is only beginning to be penetrated.

At a 500,000 potential annual market, the new method for gall bladder surgery offers a significant sales opportunity for U.S. Surgical, which sells the kit for $400 to $500 for each procedure. The potential, however, does not stop there. There are 700,000 appendectomies every year that could use this technique. There are an additional 1 million hernia operations and 1 million hysterectomies that could also benefit. It is not exaggerating to say that this new form of abdominal surgery will revolutionize these procedures.

Laser Scope, Inc. also makes a laser tool that is extremely well-suited for surgery. It is a two-frequency YAG laser that can double its frequency by use of a patented substance called KTP. This double-frequency capability allows it to be used in contact or not in contact and permits cutting and coagulating steps from the same laser with the flick of a button. While this is a potentially large market, the patent on KTP expires in 1993 and the company may face competition for the process at that point. Nevertheless, in the meantime it will generate substantial revenues as the amount of laser surgery increases.

Further technological advances are being made by one of the medical industry's most innovative companies, Alza Corporation. Alza is a company that specializes in developing new drug "delivery systems." These help get a drug to the right location, in the right amount, and at the right time. Alza has several different technologies to accomplish this and all of them are important and potentially very lucrative. Not only do they improve the therapeutic effectiveness of the drug that they work with but, additionally, they prolong the effective economic life of the drug and can sometimes increase the indications for that drug.

Alza's most important commercial breakthrough was with the product Procardia XL, a drug from Pfizer that was designed to cure angina.

The dosage regimen for Procardia was several pills a day, and in consequence, the level of Procardia in the blood was frequently unevenly distributed. Alza developed a system they call Oros that scientifically encapsulates drugs and titrates them into the system in very precise amounts. It works like hi-tech Contac.

By incorporating Procardia in its Oros system, Alza was able to develop a product that would reduce the dosage of Procardia to once a day and distribute it precisely across the 24-hour period. This product was so superior to conventional Procardia delivery that it is selling extremely well and, moreover, has gotten an additional indication for use in controlling hypertension. Alza has numerous other drugs using the Oros system before the FDA. The most prominent of these delivers Volmax, an antiasthma drug developed by Glaxo. The system allows Volmax to be taken only once a day while distributing the drug into the blood stream in a very precise way. This tends to eliminate the possibility of the amount of Volmax getting too low in the blood stream, bringing on an asthmatic attack. We expect that when it is approved it will be another extremely important and profitable drug.

Another Alza product for which we expect FDA approval shortly and that has tremendous financial promise is Actasite. Actasite uses another form of drug delivery system to create an effective cure for periodontal disease. There are 60 million people in the United States suffering from periodontal disease. However, fewer than 15 percent are ever actually treated for it; because conventional treatment is extremely painful and, at the same time, not all that effective. The Alza product is a polymer impregnated with an antibiotic. The polymer is inserted into the periodontal sack and releases antibiotics over a precise period of time. This provides an effective way to kill the bacterial infections at the heart of periodontal problems. We expect Actasite to be extremely successful. Alza has signed a direct marketing agreement with Procter & Gamble to distribute the product.

Another Alza product that could be very successful once approved is called TTS. TTS is a method of delivering testosterone transdermally and is intended for men who are impotent. It works because one of the main causes of impotence is an inadequate level of testosterone. Alza's treatment consists of a patch affixed to the scrotum. The patch releases a consistent level of testosterone transdermally. This product could be very lucrative.

Another Alza product is being developed in conjunction with Merck. Merck has a product called Ivomec that has a large sales base ($400 million) and is growing at a 20 percent to 30 percent rate. Ivomec is an extremely effective treatment against parasites in cattle. However, to administer it, the cattle have to be rounded up fairly frequently, which is difficult and expensive to do. The Alza delivery system encapsulates the Ivomec in a bolus that stays in the rumen (one of the cow's several stomachs), and continues to deliver the drug on a scientifically titrated basis over an entire grazing season.

Alza is also working on a transdermal patch that helps people to stop smoking. This product looks to be extremely effective. Presently, the company has a large number of products in review by the FDA, and it is working with many drug companies on using their patented delivery systems to extend the product lives of older drugs. We expect this company to be one of the most interesting growth stocks of the 90s.

THREE SMALL COMPANIES

Another product area that could have substantial economic importance to three small companies is in the development of effective treatments for stress incontinence. Stress incontinence affects a very large number of elderly people; it is a form of incontinence resulting in involuntary urination when the patient laughs, coughs, lifts an object, or performs strenuous physical activity. While there are operations performed on 50,000 people a year for stress incontinence, it is estimated that there is a much larger population who are addressing the problem by wearing diapers, maxipads, or not at all. It is estimated that there are perhaps 3 to 5 million adults in the United States who wear diapers.

The problem is being attacked in slightly different ways by the three companies. The first is by Mentor Corporation, which has a substantial history with a teflon-derived substance used to treat vocal cord injuries. Mentor has discovered that this product injected into the urethra causes sufficient constriction of the urethra to prevent the stress incontinence effect. It has received approval by the FDA for use in men who have had prostate surgery. Full approval is expected by 1992. It is expected that patients will pay $1,000 per treatment, so the revenue to Mentor could eventually be very substantial.

The second of these companies is Collagen, which in collaboration with C. R. Bard has a joint venture to produce a product known as Contagen. The treatment is essentially the same as Mentor's except that a collagen extract is used rather than teflon to create the constriction in the urethra. Approval is expected in late 1991 or early 1992.

Collagen may be several months behind Mentor in the approval process. Mentor has already been approved for men, a small segment of the patient population. Nevertheless, we expect both companies to get substantial revenue from this product in the 90s, providing a high level of growth. It should be mentioned that Mentor is growing at a 5 to 10 percent rate, exclusive of this product, by being the leading factor in another medical area: implants. Mentor's implants have a variety of applications, including breast implants for women who have suffered from a mastectomy or who want cosmetic enlargement and penile implants for men with total sexual dysfunction.

The third competitor, Bioplasty Inc., is planning to compete with Mentor and Collagen in the stress incontinence market. They are several years behind, however. Bioplasty does have FDA approval for a substance for use in breast implants. This substance has qualities that may make it safer than products now on the market and should make Bioplasty a rapidly growing company in the early 90s.[1]

Another new technology that is going to be a big revenue generator in the 90s is in implantable defibrillators (AIDC). An implantable defibrillator is like a pacemaker, except that a pacemaker regulates heartbeats that are too slow, whereas defibrillators stop ventricular fibrillation or overly rapid or spasmodic heartbeats. Most people are familiar with the normal defibrillator machines that are used to literally jolt patients, who have suffered heart attacks, back to life. This device accomplishes essentially the same thing, but on a much smaller scale.

Eli Lilly already has a first-generation product that has significant sales, $120 million approximately. The main breakthrough, however, will be the second-generation products that will be small enough to be comfortable to the patient and therefore find widespread application.

There are 320,000 people per year who have the potential for sudden cardiac arrest. Of these only 10 percent survive. All patients who have had a heart attack, either a myocardial infarction or congestive heart failure, are at risk of sudden cardiac arrest. Similarly, there are a large number of patients, estimated at 60,000, who are taking drugs for cardiac arrhythmias; some of them are also good candidates for this product. These products will probably

---

[1] More recently Bioplasty has run afoul of the FDA and its breast implant approval is in question.

sell for between $15,000 and $18,000 per unit (the Lilly first-generation product sells for $20,000) and will generate substantial revenues.

The two leading AICD makers, which are publicly traded, are Lilly and Medtronic. We estimate that the development of this product will enable Medtronic to grow at a 15 percent rate through much of the 90s. There are a number of other competitors, but none are publicly traded.

Another technology that may become commercially viable in late 1992/1993 is PRK (photorefractive keratectomy). PRK is the process of resculpting the shape of the eye, using lasers. The main use of this product is to cure bad eyesight although it can also be used for treatment of glaucoma and other eye diseases. The work is performed with an excimer laser that vaporizes minute quantities of the cornea with each pulse. While this sounds very frightening, only a micron or two of cell structure is actually removed with each laser pulse so that there is very little chance of substantial damage, even if the laser is not precisely aimed. Moreover, the ability to aim the laser more precisely is being developed and it appears as though this process is reasonably effective. Obviously the market size is huge; there are 140 million people in this country with corrected vision. The leader in this field is a very small company called Summit Technology although there is another company, Taunton, which is a close competitor.

There are a number of issues involving this technology to be resolved. First, the patent situation is murky. Second, there are questions as to the accuracy of correction. Eighty percent of the people are correctible to one diopter. This only assures correction to 20/50, although there are obviously many cases where the correction is perfect. Third, the process is expensive, it costs $1,500 per eye at present.

Despite these drawbacks, we believe there will be a significant number of people who will opt for this process once the technology is known to be safe and it has been approved by the FDA. As Summit Technology makes money by selling the laser equipment to ophthalmologists at $200,000 per laser, as well as selling a disposable product that is part of the process (at $100 per eye), this company could generate significant revenues from the development and acceptance of this new technology.

Another interesting company is Ballard Medical Products. Ballard was founded by Dale Ballard, a man who built up and sold another medical technology company, Deseret Pharmaceuticals. Dale Ballard has had a reputation for developing small but important medical niche products. Ballard Medical has developed several products that are important adjuncts to critical care technology. The first is the Trach (pronounced trake). This is a disposable endotracheal suction device that is used when a patient is on a ventilator. Typically, when a patient is on a ventilator his or her trachea must be cleaned out periodically. This product permits cleaning out of the trachea automatically without the removal of the ventilator. This is extremely important in that it is much faster than the conventional procedure. It is more cost effective because it requires fewer nurses to operate it.

The second product developed by Ballard Medical is a surgical soap which comes in a foam. While the product doesn't seem to be technologically sophisticated, its revenues are growing extremely rapidly. Lastly, Ballard has developed a product that is not yet being sold. This product, called Micro-trach, was developed by Dr. Heimlich (inventor of the Heimlich maneuver). It is a small device that is inserted into the throat through a needle-sized hole. Using this device, oxygen can be supplied directly to the throat rather than in the conventional manner of putting tubes up the nose. While it sounds unpleasant to have it inserted, it is a far more efficient way of providing oxygen and is apparently much more comfortable once it is installed. There are 500 thousand people who have chronic oxygen needs and there are 5 million needing some kind of oxygen support.

Ballard has an extremely good sales force oriented toward the hospital community and is constantly producing small niche products to fill needs as they develop. As a consequence, the company is growing very rapidly as did its predecessor, Deseret Pharmaceuticals.

Another company worthy of note is Molecular Biosystems. It has developed the first contrast agent for ultrasound. A contrast agent is a substance that is typically injected into the body to permit imaging machinery to see a target organ more precisely. While there are contrast agents of various kinds for X rays, CAT scans and MRIs, there is no effective contrast agent for ultrasound. Molecular Biosystems is a company created to sell a product that was developed by a Dr. Feinstein, a renowned cardiologist from the University of Chicago. Patented in 1986, the product is based on albumen, a substance that occurs naturally in the blood; it is known as "sonicated albumen" and goes by the trade name Albunex.

Presently, the best way to see the heart is to make an angiogram. To do this a contrast agent is injected into the heart through a catheter. This is a very unpleasant procedure as the catheter is usually placed into a blood vessel and fed all the way to the heart. The contrast agent then permits the heart's functioning to be seen by an imaging machine. When Albunex is approved a simple injection will accomplish much the same thing.

Used in conjunction with ultrasound, Albunex will provide clarity in those 25 percent of endocardiograms that are not presently clear enough. Usually, this occurs because conventional ultrasound cannot really see the endocardial borders well enough. While effectiveness data has not been released on Albunex, we believe that it will show a dramatic increase in endocardiogram effectiveness. Molecular Biosystems has marketing agreements with three very powerful contrast agent companies, Hafslund Nycomed (a Norwegian company which has European rights), Mallinckrodt (USA), and Shionogi (Japan). Albunex has other imaging applications and we expect that by the time all of its possible applications are added together it will dramatically increase the effectiveness of ultrasound and also provide extremely large profit potential for the company in the 90s.

It should be mentioned, however, that Albunex requires a PMA from the FDA in order to go on the market. (A PMA is an approval for a device.) It is expected that the PMA approval could come as early as October 1, 1991. Until such time there will be minimal earnings for the company. However, once the product is approved, we expect the earnings to build up rapidly.

Another area of promise is the development bone densometers. As I mentioned in Chapter 7 concerning Merck, there are probably over 20 million people who have osteoporosis. Osteoporosis is an extremely difficult and dangerous disease of the aged. The disease essentially causes the bones to become thinner and more fragile. This can frequently result in bone fractures, especially of the hip, which are painful, extremely expensive to treat, and sometimes fatal. It is a disease that strikes, with great frequency, postmenopausal women, especially women of small physical stature. Presently treatments for this disease are not very effective. Women have been treated with estrogen, but this treatment has raised questions concerning possible carcinogenic effect. Others are treated with calcitonin. However, to date, this treatment has not been that effective. A new class of drugs known as diphosphonates seem to have some promise. This includes Procter & Gamble's product Didronal, which should be approved next year, and is the first substantial advance against this disease. Many people are working on more advanced drugs, Merck included.

Because new treatments will become available, the bone densometer looks like a machine that could generate substantial revenues. The primary manufacturers of this product are Hologic and another company, called Lunar. We believe at present that the Hologic machine is slightly superior as it does not require manual calibration. These machines are used to measure accurately the density of the bones. A baseline for each is established and then the bones are measured periodically; this determines whether the patient is developing osteoporosis and also whether the patient is responding to treatment. Because the treatments for this disease are becoming much more sophisticated and effective, there is now a much greater need for measuring devices to assess the level of the illness in any individual patient. We expect both Hologic and Lunar to develop substantial sales of this product and have rapid revenue growth as a result.

Interestingly, there is a vitamin, which is a form of vitamin D (vitamin 1 Alpha D3) that seems to be effective in combating osteoporosis. This vitamin has been used in Japan, but because the American diet makes it toxic for Americans, not here. Lunar, however, is working on a variant of the vitamin that may have potential in the mid-90s. Presently most of Hologics sales occur in Europe, where treatment is more advanced. The American market remains untapped.

We have discussed several medical technologies that we find interesting. Others will doubtless emerge during the decade. This industry is a fascinating one and replete with growth stocks that have great potential for the 90s. The economic characteristics found among medical technology stocks are compelling. They include: (*a*) rapidly growing markets, (*b*) comparative freedom from overseas competition, and (*c*) inelastic price structures for most products, leading to the potential for aggressive pricing and consequently high margins.

KEY INVESTMENT POINTS

1. Generally, these companies may grow very rapidly during the 90s because of the strong growth of the industry. However, individual companies may or may not grow rapidly, depending on their products.

2. Companies supplying medical technologies may or may not have to get FDA approval for their products. Sometimes the rules change. An investor should know these facts (e.g., Bioplasty).

3. Some medical technology companies' products require marketing to doctors, hospitals, or other health care professionals; this

requires a sophisticated well-trained sales force. An investor should be aware of a company's marketing capability and reputation. It is always wise to consult with doctors or the relevant specialist on these points.

4. Companies whose products save money versus an alternate course of therapy will make headway in the 90s. New cost-saving techniques such as the laparoscopic cholecystectomy will be very exciting growth areas.

5. Some companies in medical technology can grow extremely fast (40 percent), but the stocks can be very volatile. Beware of any product disappointments.

CHAPTER 9

MEDICAL COST CONTAINMENT

One of the most noticeable aspects of the coming medical cost spiral is that it will place an increasing burden on parties that have to reimburse for health care—Medicare, Medicaid, private insurance plans, and, of course, individuals. During the 90s a great effort will be made to contain costs that will appear to be increasingly out of control. It is possible that new government laws or regulations may alter the profitability of various industries in an effort to control the cost spiral. An investor should be aware of this possibility.

In practice, there is a trade-off between superior health care quality and inexpensive health care. In America, the medical establishment is dedicated to curing all prevailing diseases, regardless of cost. There is no acceptance of triage; it is part of our moral philosophy that any patient that can be cured should be cured no matter what the cost. Frequently, however, the solution to difficult medical problems is extremely expensive at the margin. Some of the newer products and techniques that we have discussed are going to greatly improve the prognosis for a number of serious diseases but, at the same time, they are going to be extremely expensive.

An example of this is Genentech's TPA, which costs $2,000 a dose. Of course, there are positive therapeutic trade-offs. Some drugs such as TPA, Centecor's Centoxin, and the colony stimulating factors are expensive, but result in a substantially reduced hospital stays and in the end may be more cost effective than conventional treatment.

COST CONTAINMENT

Despite the trade-offs, newer medical technology is going to contribute to the rising nominal cost of health care in the 90s. However, effort is being made to control these costs and this has spawned companies that attempt to provide health care in a more cost-effective manner. I have lumped these together in a category called *medical cost containment*. There are numerous companies in this category and several of them deserve to be mentioned because they are going to grow rapidly in the 90s. In many cases, these companies will be replacing older, conventional ways of providing care.

The first of these efforts is the at-home pharmacy industry, dominated by one company, Medco Containment Services. Medco Containment Services is an extremely interesting and fast-growing company. Its primary business is selling drugs through the mail. Typically, this service is designed for people needing treatment for chronic diseases. Medco orients its activity, however, not toward individuals but toward funded medical plans. It provides several services. It functions as a benefits consultant; it also designs and operates drug plans, sending the drugs, and processing the claims for the sponsor.

A typical client might be a corporation that is self-insuring its health plan. Medco will come to the corporation and design a program whereby individuals within the plan can get their drugs through the mail more cheaply than at a drug store. This, of course, involves a number of things, including prescribing more generics in place of prescription drugs as well as eliminating some of the dispensing fees charged by the typical neighborhood pharmacy.

It is part of Medco's responsibility to sell the service to the individuals within the plan. They send pamphlets and advertise to the members and then provide an integrated computer-detailed view of drug activity to the sponsor. This gives the plan's sponsor an overview to determine if any plan members are abusing or using an excessive level of drugs. Obviously, this saves money; it saves the corporate sponsor money because they are obligated, under many typical formulas, to reimburse the individual who needs the drug. It also saves the individual money because he usually has some form of co-payment with the plan and this is reduced by the use of less expensive drugs. It is also convenient for the individual member, especially if he is using chronic medication; he receives his medication through the mail.

The growth of this company has been spectacular. New members have been growing at 10 percent to 15 percent a year and current members have been increasing their utilization of the program about 20 percent on top of that. Moreover, there has been a 7 percent to 10 percent increase in the prices of prescriptions, and since newer medicines are also more expensive there is an upward bias for revenues to Medco. Consequently, Medco's revenues have been growing at a very high rate and we expect this to continue. Presently, the total industry sales for at-home pharmacy services is estimated to be about $2 billion; Medco clearly dominates this market, having sales of $1 billion. Despite its rapid growth, Medco still has significant growth potential; 70 percent of the Fortune 500 have no at-home pharmacy mail plan. In fact, Medco has only penetrated about 11 percent of the Fortune 500.

Moreover, only 65 percent of Blue Cross/Blue Shield plans and only 50 percent of the top insurance companies have this option. It is operative in only 14 states.

It is estimated that a Medco plan can save its customers 20 percent to 30 percent on its pharmacy costs. Already Medco is Merck's largest customer, and relationships like this provide substantial price leverage. We believe this company can grow very rapidly in the future.

OUTPATIENT CENTERS

Another area of great potential growth is the rehabilitation market. Presently, rehabilitation is a $10 billion market growing at 20 percent a year. Rehabilitation encompasses therapy after car accidents, therapy for stroke victims, post-surgical rehabilitation, and so forth. Presently, this is done as an adjunct service of conventional mainstream hospitals. However, providing rehabilitation in a conventional hospital is extremely expensive because the rehabilitation wing has to incur its portion of the overhead cost of the whole hospital. Nevertheless, this is a very large industry and a growing one.

Recently, independent freestanding rehabilitation companies have come into their own as businesses. Probably the foremost example is Healthsouth Rehabilitation. Healthsouth provides two types of independent rehabilitation facilities. First, it runs inpatient facilities inside hospitals for those requiring round-the-clock care. More importantly, they have a very rapidly growing chain of outpatient centers that they call CORFs, for Comprehensive Outpatient Rehabilitation Facilities. CORFs are designed to accommodate rehabilitation in a nonhospital setting for patients who are able to get to the facility on their own. CORFs are far less expensive than the same facility in a hospital. At the same time, they are designed exclusively for rehabilitation and so the facilities are frequently superior. Also, because the staff members are trained specifically in rehabilitation the care may be better.

In general, many employers are finding that paying for rehabilitation is a cost-effective process. Some studies have shown that $1 spent on rehab saves $11 to $30 on future employee benefits, workmens' compensation costs, and absenteeism.

Another company that reduces health care costs by providing an outpatient alternative to hospitals is Medical Care International, which operates freestanding outpatient surgery centers. Again, the objective is reduction in the cost of treatment compared to that supplied by hospitals. The concept is to move surgical procedures that can be done on an outpatient basis away from hospitals to facilities that are better equipped to handle them and that do not have to absorb the general overhead associated with acute care hospitals.

Surgical procedures performed in Medical Care's centers cost 25 percent to 30 percent less than those done in hospital outpatient departments. A substantial and growing number of procedures can be performed on an outpatient basis. This is because of the great strides being made in medical technology, allowing more complex surgery to be performed outside of an acute care hospital setting.

Advances in less-invasive procedures that we discussed in Chapter 8 and improvements in anesthesiology will enable much more complicated cases to be handled in freestanding centers. The case load will broaden, increasing the growth of Medical Care and similar companies. Gall bladder surgery, which we discussed in Chapter 8, is an example of a new high-revenue operation that can now be done on an outpatient basis.

The market for surgery centers is very large and the penetration is small. In 1989 there were approximately 41.6 million operations performed in the United States of which only 2.2 million were performed in freestanding units and 11.3 million were performed in the outpatient wing of conventional hospitals. Obviously, not all operations lend themselves to outpatient surgical centers; serious operations, such as cardiac surgery require prolonged hospital stays. However, it is estimated that 60 percent or more can be performed on an outpatient basis. Thus, freestanding surgical centers have a big potential market. They have significant cost advantages over the outpatient wing of acute care hospitals, and the number of outpatient procedures will increase rapidly as a percentage of all operations.

In the previous chapter we discussed a variety of new technologies that are going to enable complex operations to be performed in a manner that dramatically reduces the time of recovery. Lasers and endoscopy techniques permit surgery that is much less damaging to the body, and consequently the recuperative time is reduced in many cases, allowing operations that formerly took three or four days recovery time to be performed on an outpatient basis. These new devices will accelerate the demand for outpatient surgery facilities so that it is estimated, by the mid-90s, over half of all operations performed in the United States will be done on an outpatient basis.

DRUG TESTING

Another interesting growth area that is not strictly medical, but fits into this chapter because of avoided medical costs is drug testing. Illegal drug use causes significant medical costs due to accidents in the workplace. Moreover, it causes significant absenteeism and loss of productivity. Additionally, drug rehabilitation programs are expensive and add to medical costs. There is no question but that a large amount of medical costs, as well as reduced productivity, is associated with the use of illegal drugs in the workplace in the United States. The latest studies show 18 percent of workers are drug-compromised. This is an extremely complex issue that has no specific solution, but the medical costs that will occur from drug use in the 90s will be very great.

Presently, in New York City, the majority of new AIDS cases relates not to homosexual activity, but to intravenous drug use. Thus, from an employer's point of view, the cost associated with drugs in the workplace will be an important added pressure to medical costs during this decade.

The legal complexities surrounding drug testing would require an entire book to explore thoroughly. However, the purpose of this book is to identify growth areas of the future pertaining to the stock market, and certainly drug testing is one. A company that we find potentially interesting in this endeavor is Psychemedics, a small company with extremely modest revenues at present. However, it has a technology with the potential to grow rapidly as drug testing expands. Presently, most employers use drug testing, not for screening their existing population of workers (which involves significant legal complexities), but for identifying drug use among job applicants. This is cynically described as "letting your competitors have the drug addicts." Psychemedics has an interesting testing technique, different from the conventional method, urinalysis.

Psychemedics tests strands of hair, rather than urine. A government agency known as National Institute on Drug Abuse (NIDA) has officially sanctioned the use of urine samples as a way of testing for drugs. It has not yet sanctioned the method used by Psychemedics. Indeed there is some resistance on the part of the government to endorse the Psychemedics technique and, additionally, there has been no court case to confirm its effectiveness. However, we believe the Psychemedics technique to be superior to urinalysis.

As the method requires using 60 strands of hair, a reasonable clump, it is not totally clear whether an employee would prefer to be tested by urinalysis, which involves urinating in front of a witness, or surrendering a clump of hair. However, the hair-cutting technique is superior as far as detecting drug addiction. The reason for this is simple: the body expunges all signs of drug ingestion within several days and, consequently, urinalysis is not effective in determining whether a potential employee took drugs a week or a month before. The hair technique, however, reveals any traces of drugs within the past three months and can test for five major drug groups; opiates (heroin), cocaine, marijuana, meth-amphetamines, and PCP. Any positive readings using either method are generally confirmed by a liquid gas chromotography test, in any case. The Psychemedics test is more expensive but it does identify a much larger number of drug addicts and is therefore more effective. We believe that this company and, possibly other similar companies will become a major industry in the 90s as business attempts to avert the medical costs and productivity loss associated with drugs in the workplace. It should be noted that Psychemedics has limited financial resources and substantial analysis should be made before investing in the stock.

HOME INFUSION THERAPY

Another industry that is growing rapidly is the home infusion therapy industry. Home infusion therapy began in 1982 with the pioneering efforts of companies such as Caremark, now a division of Baxter. Over the last decade the number of treatable conditions has increased threefold from 300 to 900 and the home infusion industry has grown to $1.5 billion and continues to expand very rapidly. This business's purpose is similar to others we have discussed, reduction of medical costs by moving therapy out of the hospitals. The theory is that treatment at home is much less expensive than hospital care as well as being preferred by the patient. In this procedure treatment involves infusing drugs, nutrients, or fluids into the body intravenously or through a feeding tube, targeted at a variety of chronic conditions.

Typically, this kind of therapy begins in the hospital with doctors prescribing a course of treatment (known as a "protocol") for the patient. Nurses work with the patient (and/or another family member) to teach him how to operate the equipment to infuse solutions into his body. When the patient goes home, a company representative comes to the house and sets up the apparatus for infusion; this includes the delivery mechanisms as well as refrigerators to store drugs. Subsequently, depending on the illness and the protocol, a nurse will come, anywhere from one time per day to once a month, to either help the patient with his therapy or to provide monitoring as the patient accomplishes his own therapy.

There are several major classifications of home infusion therapies. These are, in order of size:

1. Total parenteral nutrition (TPN). This accounts for approximately one third of the $1.5 billion total industry sales. It is oriented toward patients unable to digest food. A catheter is installed in the patient's upper digestive tract and he receives nutrition through this catheter. There are several diseases that make patients unable to eat conventionally: these are Crohn's disease, acute colitis, Hirschsprung's disease, a variety of cancers, and AIDS.

2. Antibiotics therapy. This accounts for one quarter of industry sales and is growing extremely rapidly as home infusion lends itself nicely to acute antibiotic treatment. The course of therapy typically ranges from three weeks to four months and for a wide variety of severe infections, such as pneumonia, endocarditis, Lyme's disease, and infections resulting from AIDS. Several other rapidly growing uses are in chemotherapy, pain management, and treatments for other AIDS complications.

Presently the largest company in the home infusion industry remains the Caremark division of Baxter, which has over 35 percent share of the market. Following Caremark are Critical Care of America, Inc., Home Nutritional Services, and T-Square Medical. This industry is growing extremely rapidly and there is a proliferation of new companies entering the business. The barriers to entry are low, and receivables management tends to be a prerequisite for success.

Any potential investor should be aware that, because of the low barriers to entry in this industry, there will inevitably be a shakeout.

However, at the moment, the major publicly owned companies are all growing extremely rapidly without competing with one another in a pernicious way.

HMOs

No chapter on medical cost containment would be complete without some mention of Health Maintenance Organizations, otherwise known as HMOs. HMOs are actually a disparate group of cost-containment planning organizations that were developed in the early 80s and have been growing in a sporadic way since then. There are many forms of HMOs, which are listed in Figure 9–1. However, the concept is that the employers's plan insures the individual, but at the same time mandates that, to some extent, the individual has to use services, hospitals, or doctors of a specific type. Obviously, the indemnity type that is listed in the chart does not require that the patient use any particular doctor or any hospital. However, at the other end of the spectrum are staff model HMOs that have not only their own hospitals but have doctors under contract. This permits HMOs to obtain doctors more inexpensively and also permits a great deal of cost control on the part of the plan. There are, as the chart indicates, many gradations in between.

It is small wonder the HMOs have become as successful as they are. Presently 35 million people are enrolled in HMOs compared with 14 million in 1983. While the growth has slowed, HMOs will continue to grow in the 90s. The impetus for this is the fact that, as of the present, approximately half of all pre-tax profits of American corporations are going toward providing health care benefits and there is an acceleration in health care costs.

Presently, it is estimated that 30 percent of all group health plans are involved in HMOs as opposed to 4 percent in 1980. When HMOs first emerged in the early 80s they grew extraordinarily until about 1986. There were 250 HMOs in 1982; there were 650 by the mid-80s.

During the early to mid-80s there were many large and well-managed HMO organizations which took root. Unfortunately, there were also a large number of undercapitalized organizations that were simply glorified insurance plans. The industry was so unsaturated that to start an HMO in the mid-80s, required little effort or capital. An entrepreneur had to create an insurance plan to cover the beneficiaries and then go out and make

FIGURE 9–1
Managed Medical Plans Save Money

Type of Plan	What It Offers	Method of Cost Control	Advantages to Patient	Disadvantages	Monthly Premium* (Annual inflation rate)
		LESS COST CONTROL			
Indemnity	Services from any doctor or hospital	None except screening for fraudulent claims	Choice of any doctor or hospital	Claim forms to file; preventive services not covered	$382 24%
Indemnity with Utilization Review	Services from any doctor or hospital	Prior approval required for hospitalization and certain outpatient procedures	Choice of any doctor and access to any hospital, after prior approval	Additional paperwork to get approval of some services; preventive services not covered	$371 23%
Preferred Provider Organization	Services from any doctor or hospital, but at lower cost to employee using network	Discounts negotiated with hospitals and doctors; prior approval required for hospitalization and some outpatient procedures	Higher rate of reimbursement within network	Lower reimbursement outside network; additional paperwork to get approval of some services; preventive services not covered	$366 21%

FIGURE 9–1 (continued)

Type of Plan	What It Offers	Method of Cost Control	Advantages to Patient	Disadvantages	Monthly Premium* (Annual inflation rate)
		MORE COST CONTROL			
Open health Maintenance Organization	Services from any doctor or hospital, but at lower cost to employee using network	Within network, family doctors manage utilization of services; hospital and physician fees are discounted	Within network, lower co-payments; preventive care covered; no claims forms	Higher cost for services outside network	$354 16%
HMO with independent doctors (IPA)	Services from any hospital or independent doctor affiliated with HMO	Family doctors manage services; hospital and physician fees are discounted	Low co-payments; preventive care covered; no claim forms	Must use approved doctors and hospitals	$325 13%
HMO with staff doctors	Services from hospitals under contract with HMO or salaried doctors at its medical centers	Family doctors at HMO medical centers manage services; hospital and physician fees are discounted	Low co-payments; preventive care covered; no claim forms	Must use medical center doctors and approved hospitals	$292 10%

* Nationwide average family premium paid to insurer, including any portion paid by employee.

FIGURE 9-1 (concluded)
.. And Are Winning Market Share

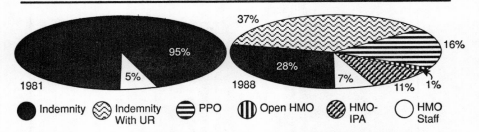

Cigna's spectrum of health plans (table) shows that as managerial control tightens, costs and the anticipated inflation rate shrink impressively. In 1981, aside from a small number in staff, group, and other HMOs, all U.S. workers were in unmanaged "indemnity" health plans; today fewer than half are.

contracts with doctors and hospitals to provide the service. Unfortunately, there was little appreciation of the degree to which health care costs would rise by the late 80s and, as a consequence, medical loss ratios rose dramatically. A number of early HMOs suffered dramatic reversals as a result. Maxicare, once the largest publicly owned HMO, went bankrupt.

Also, John Hancock, Transamerica, Firemen's Fund, and Allstate Insurance companies all withdrew from the HMO business. Other large insurance companies—CIGNA, Aetna, and Prudential-Bache—reorganized their plans. After the shakeout, health insurance prices increased substantially; they soared 16 percent to 20 percent in 1989 and profitability once again returned to the industry.

At present, it appears that the HMOs that will be successful in the 90s are either those with nationwide capability or an extremely strong regional presence. The ability to directly provide some of the services is also important, as is overall cost control and delivery of high quality medical service. Probably the best and largest pure HMO is Kaiser Permanente, a California-based giant whose membership jumped by a record 600,000 in 1989 to a total 6.2 million. Kaiser has one of the most profitable formulas; is a staff model HMO that employs its own doctors and owns its own facilities. Unfortunately, Kaiser is not a public company.

Another example of a staff model HMO that has been very successful, and has been growing, is FHP International, also located in California. A third staff model HMO that looks to have a bright future is located in Nevada; it is called Sierra Health Services. Foundation Health Corporation and HMO America are two others worth considering. Yet again another viable contender in this market is Humana, which has a large chain of acute care hospitals, but also is an HMO provider.

The HMO industry experienced its most rapid growth in the 80s. Nevertheless, there will be some companies, such as the ones just mentioned, which will benefit from corporate cost containment practices and as a consequence, will grow in the 90s as well.

Presently, there is some debate whether Health Care Financing Administration (HCFA), which regulates the pricing for Medicare reimbursement for HMOs, is going to continue to provide an adequate level of rate increases in this time of budgetary austerity. It is our belief that the government has a distinct desire to push Medicare recipients toward HMOs and consequently is not going to discourage them by providing inadequate price relief. Overall, HMOs will continue to supply an accelerating piece of the American health care market both from the public and private payment sectors.

Another company that has experienced very rapid growth is HealthCare COMPARE. HealthCare COMPARE is similar to an HMO in that it enables corporations to achieve the lowest cost health care. However, HealthCare COMPARE merely provides comparative data on health care procedures, enabling companies to reduce costs by evaluating the efficiency of its providers. It is able also to direct its clients toward cost-reducing formats such as PPOs. PPOs are preferred providers. These function like HMOs but are merely consortia of doctors and facilities and do not provide the health insurance aspect.

HealthCare COMPARE is extremely profitable because it does not bear the costs of providing the care itself. Nevertheless, it is growing extremely rapidly because corporations find that they need an objective standard against which to measure their expenditures. We expect this company to grow rapidly in the 90s.

KEY INVESTMENT POINTS

1. Containing medical costs will be an obsession in the 1990s. Companies that provide alternate (cheaper) forms of therapy will grow rapidly during the decade.

2. An investor should fully understand the service the company is offering and how it compares to conventional formats.

3. Many of these companies are chains, similar to fast-food chains. Be aware of the ''store opening'' schedule.

4. An investor should understand the barriers to entry in the business. Some are regulatory, some relate to the availability of trained professionals. If barriers are low, competition will develop sooner or later; if high, then growth may be curtailed.

5. Some HMOs own their own facilities and employ their own doctors. Some, however, are really just health insurance plans. When premiums are rising faster than costs, few industries grow faster, but there is a competitive cycle and HMO stocks can be devastated on the downswing. Beware of this cycle, it has broken hearts and companies.

CHAPTER 10

HOW TO INVEST IN MEDICAL STOCKS

There is a saying on Wall Street, "a rising tide floats all boats." This means that if the general direction of the market or the industry in which you have invested is up, your stocks will probably go up as well. The tide will be rising very fast for medical growth stocks in the 90s. First, I believe the market as a whole will be rising. Secondly, growth stocks will be rising faster than the market. Third, stocks in the medical area, which are growing rapidly, may outperform other forms of growth stocks. This certainly was the case in 1990; medically oriented stocks were among the best performers.

Growth companies in the medical area have some unique properties that I have discussed in preceding chapters. To review, they have the following advantages:

1. They have a defined market for their products. Unlike other kinds of companies that frequently have to create the demand for their products by advertising or other marketing techniques, medical companies have a clearly defined demand; there is a large and aging population in this country, which has specific illnesses. Some of these illnesses are so severe that people will pay extremely high prices (relative to their own economic level) in order to be cured.

2. The relative ease of entry common in other high-growth industries is not as much a factor in many industries related to medicine. In the case of the drug industry, the product typically has to be approved by the Food & Drug Administration, a process that takes anywhere from 5 to 15 years. Patents are available for many pharmaceuticals and serve as effective barriers to entry. Other restrictive laws exist such as the Orphan Drug Act. Also, medical technology can be very complicated and requires a substantial amount of research spending. Lastly, marketing medical products must be done in a very sophisticated way as it is directed toward a highly intelligent decision-making population (doctors).

3. There is very little competition from overseas. The United States dominates the medical field and it will continue to do so in the 90s; an investor does not have to be concerned about excessive competition from Japan or other countries.

4. Yet another positive is that prices tend to be relatively inelastic. A modest improvement in a medical procedure can result in a very large improvement in the price of the product relative to other similar products. For this reason margins tend to be very high.

All of these factors make the medical area extraordinarily exciting from an investor's viewpoint. The aging population and the rising cost of medical care will result in substantial expenditures over the course of the 90s. This will create a large variety of potentially interesting stock choices.

I have indicated areas of the medical arena that seem like promising zones for investment exploration. Some companies will, at various times, be good investments, depending on the state of the market and individual stock valuation, and so forth.

There are some guidelines that an investor should follow when looking at medical stocks. The first is to understand the **need** that the considered company's product is attempting to serve. This is especially important in medical stocks. Talking to specialized trade associations can be extremely useful. It is also very important to know precisely the size of the patient population for the product that the company is selling or developing. Almost everybody has a family doctor, and doctors notoriously love the stock market. Potential investors should try to find a friendly and informed doctor, preferably one in the specialty in question. Ask him how many patients there are in the population; how they are presently being treated; how effective the present drugs are; and what their side effects are. Then a comparison should be made between the product of the company in question and the products currently on the market.

If a new product looks promising, it is important to follow the **progress** of the drug or product through the FDA and know when it is going to come on the market. Generally, one should not invest much more than a couple of years before the product is approved unless it is a potential blockbuster. The stock market is quite impatient and will only tolerate stocks that have no earnings for short periods of time and under specific conditions. Thus it is, generally speaking, better to invest in a company when its product is near approval.

To assess the **market size** of a potential product, one has to establish how many patients there are and find out from the company what they expect to charge, more or less, for the treatment in question. It is important to keep aware of Medicare reimbursement rates if the company plans to charge a high price. It is possible that Medicare, an increasingly important source of revenue in medicine, might not be willing to go along with reimbursing at that level. This will cause ultimately a decline in the price of the product or service.

By multiplying the price of the product by the number of patients in the population, one can determine the **ultimate size** of the market. From this, estimating revenues is often frustrating because even the best drug will penetrate its market very slowly. For example, TPA and other similar drugs we have discussed have penetrated the market for MI-type heart attacks at a lethargic rate. One would think that in the case of a drug that has a potential for saving lives, the entire patient population would get the drug right away. Unfortunately, this is not the way the medical world works. It takes a number of years before the majority of doctors accept and use a new medicine. This is why companies with strong detail forces have an advantage. If the company is a small company, it is important to know how the drug will be distributed. Frequently, a drug will be distributed through a large powerful organization which will then give a licensing fee or royalty back to the originating company.

It is impossible to give precise guidelines on how quickly a market will be penetrated. This will of course depend on how good the drug is, how good the competitive drugs are, and how serious the illness is. It is important, however, to make some assumptions in that regard to develop a good revenue forecast for the future.

It is generally true that the margin of profits on drugs can be extremely high. For biotechnology products, 80 percent of the sales dollar can come down to gross profit. Most companies, however, even small ones, invest a substantial amount of gross profit back into R&D to create new products. Also, most drug companies incur significant S.G.&A (selling general and administrative) expenses because, if they have new products they usually try to increase their sales force to sell it. Once an investor gets a sense of these numbers, however, it is possible to overlay, on the company's current results, projections about the increase in profits generated by the company's new product.

Once a new drug is approved, it is important to monitor the progress of the drug. There are services that actually give precise prescription data.

However, these services are extraordinarily expensive and an individual investor would be swamped in detail if he attempted to get this material. Most of the big brokerage firms, however, subscribe to these services and, consequently, these numbers are available to their drug analysts. By querying a drug analyst at a large brokerage firm, it is possible to ascertain how well the product in question is doing, even for smaller companies.

By overlaying the company's prospects from the various drugs that it has in its pipeline on its existing result, it is possible to build a fairly good model of the growth of revenues and profit for the target company. From there an extrapolation of earnings per share can be derived. Then, by following the valuation techniques we discussed in Chapter 3 it is possible to decide whether the stock is appropriately priced.

Companies that are not in the drug industry but are in the medical area can be approached in much the same way. It is important for the investor to recognize that these companies are selling products to a definable patient population. It is usually possible to evaluate the size of the market no matter what part of the medical arena one is analyzing. An investor should look for companies where the number of patients in the population is extremely large in relation to the size of the company; this will provide ample opportunity for the company to grow. Also the company's product should be either solving a problem for a substantial number of patients or alternatively, solving a problem that causes sufficient distress that a high price can be charged. Sometimes obscure medical areas can be wonderful hunting grounds; Amgen's EPO, for example, addresses a market that is generally unknown to the layman. Centoxin could be a very important drug even though gram negative sepsis is virtually unmentioned in the popular media.

One of the pitfalls involved in owning medical stocks is that the number of trade publications frequently publish articles reporting new side effects of popular drugs. These reports can frequently cause sharp and unanticipated drops in medical stocks. When a medical stock starts to drop rapidly, the investor should contact an analyst in a responsible brokerage firm to ascertain if there is some article of a negative nature in the trade press. Frequently, however, the effect of these articles tends to blow over and the stocks return to their pre-article levels. Good buying opportunities are sometimes created in this way.

There are also a number of medical conferences during the year and these can cause abrupt short-term movements in both direction in individual stocks. It is impossible to invest in medical stocks without a fair amount of specific knowledge about the products in question. These conferences provide this knowledge to analysts who can abruptly change their view on a specific security. Help should be sought from either a good analyst at a responsible brokerage firm or, alternatively, from a friend in the medical profession (a doctor is best) who can explain the various products on the market and note which ones have promise. Remember, however, that doctors, highly trained though they are, may not be current on the latest technology or may have ingrained prejudices.

One way to avoid the vexation of doing analysis in a rapidly changing environment is to put money in a mutual fund that specializes in medical stocks. Another choice is to put money in a diversified mutual fund that will have a reasonably high percentage in medical stocks. This partly spoils the fun but frequently can produce better results for the individual investor, as a very substantial amount of sophisticated technical knowledge is required to make successful investments.

If you want to begin investing in this field and are starting from scratch, however, I suggest that you take the products and companies that I have mentioned and explore them thoroughly. I have not discussed all the stocks that will be interesting, nor do all the companies I have mentioned have interesting stocks. They represent a good departure point for someone just beginning.

Last, I should add a caveat. The rising cost of health care as well as the fact that some 30 million Americans have no health insurance is causing a great deal of political activity. This activity may result in legislation that will reduce the profitability of some of the groups we discussed. While sweeping changes are unlikely, concern about governmental interference could have a psychological effect on companies, groups, or the whole medical arena. An investor should always remember that the government hates to see people getting rich and be sensitive to political events.

CHAPTER 11

DATA PROCESSING KEEPS ON GROWING

Data processing technology has provided many great growth stock investments since the 1960s and will be one of the most interesting areas in which to invest over the next eight years.

Data processing technology refers to the electronic transfer and manipulation of data. This is generally accomplished by computers, but is aided by a variety of related and ancillary equipment such as storage devices, modems, software, and phone equipment. Most people visualize computers as large boxes in air-conditioned rooms, performing very rapid batch calculations; this type of computer is called a mainframe. In most corporations this type of computer is used to handle big processing jobs such as accounting and payroll; they are also typically used for engineering and scientific applications. By the 1990s, however, this limited concept of a computer or computing has broken down substantially. There are various new types of devices taking over jobs normally assigned to the big mainframes that we associated with the term *computer*.

Computers surround us. One special application computer, Nintendo, has found its way into millions of American homes, although most people don't think of it as a computer. In other places computers are camouflaged behind different names; "workstations" and "laptops" are merely two types of computers. Smaller computers, such as the two just mentioned as well as those referred to as "PCs," are becoming much more powerful and are taking over jobs formerly accomplished by mainframes. Another term, *servers*, is being referred to more frequently in networked data processing systems.

The nature of computing has changed as well. In prior decades computing was something primarily accomplished in corporate data processing departments. These consisted of a variety of experts who presided over the computer resources. Computers required complex programming skills and a variety of engineering capabilities; ordinary executives rarely become involved with them. Now many, if not most, executives use computers in one form or another. Higher level languages and programs have been developed so that programming is much less arcane.

Television commercials now depict computers as so easy to use that they require very limited instruction. Computers are now so simple from a human interface standpoint that they are accessible to just about everybody in an office. By the age of 10, children are conversant with the basics of computing and completely at home with a computer keyboard. Most college students use a small computer for word processing, if not other forms of analysis. Laptop computers have made computers easy to carry around. They are today what calculators were in the 1970s.

Today, functionality is now being expressed in terms of vertical markets. Hardware and software packages are designed specifically for applications oriented toward smaller niche businesses. The computer printout has become ubiquitous in our society.

There is no question that data processing in its new expanded form is going to continue to be one of the fastest-growing industries in the country and the world. As such, it deserves a great deal of attention as a marketplace for interesting growth stocks. Unlike the medical area, however, investing in data processing stocks contains a number of pitfalls that should be recognized. Change in data processing technology is extraordinarily rapid. New products frequently only have a six-month product cycle. Often, companies obsolete even their own products at a dizzying rate. When companies have a gap between one product and another (a period known in Wall Street jargon as a product transition), corporate earnings can frequently fall dramatically and stocks can fall even more rapidly. Despite what we may think, barriers to entry in the computer/data processing business are not that great. It is obviously extremely difficult to design a semiconductor chip, also difficult is the design of a computer. Nevertheless, there are many people in this country as well as in others (principally Japan) who are able to perform these tasks. I often find myself reminding our analysts that just because *they* can't design a computer themselves doesn't mean that there aren't thousands of engineers pouring out of universities such as MIT who can. Therefore, barriers to entry are lower than might be assumed.

Computer manufacturing requires a substantial input of capital. However, many companies have sufficient capital to stay competitive. In some cases, the rapid evolution of technology, combined with the large capital requirements and the need to maintain substantial R&D, suppresses return on equity. Also, small increments in terms of perform- ance are frequently not rewarded by big increments in price as they are in the medical field. Indeed a characteristic of this business is that prices of products are constantly declining versus the capability that they generate. It can be truly said that data processing is one of the few industries in the world where the price–value relationship is consistently falling. In a sense, it represents the purest form of deflation, from the consumer's point of view.

Despite all these hazards there are very significant growth opportuni- ties in some of these companies. Several of the best growth stocks of the last decade, Compaq and Apple, we have already mentioned. A company that we will mention later in greater detail is Conner Peripherals, which over the past five years has been the fastest-growing large public company in America. The pitfalls inherent in investing in data processing stock are many, varied, and can be severe, but a lot of money can be made by plac- ing bets correctly.

Before we discuss individual investments, let me review the techno- logical changes that have brought computing to its current status. I plan to use as little technical jargon as possible. Technological understanding of data processing is not required to make successful investments in these stocks. However, certain rudiments should be understood in order to grasp the significance of the trends taking place.

The primary change from which the technological improvements of the last decade derived is the availability of much more powerful inte- grated circuits. Computer hardware (the machine itself) is basically little more than a box with a number of powerful integrated circuits inside. These integrated circuits are arranged on printed circuit boards (PCB) that are flat pieces of laminated material with imbedded electrical connectors designed to have integrated circuits mounted on them. No matter how big a computer is one can open the box and find a rack of PC boards all con- nected to each other by wires.

Integrated circuits are also known as semiconductors, or chips. They are fingernail-size pieces of equipment on which are etched all the cir- cuitry required to perform specific functions. The circuitry is created by specifically applying various materials to a base of silicon, thereby creating little circuits. These little circuits, which are microscopic, contain the logic from which a computer is built.

There are essentially several basic kinds of integrated circuits. There are memory chips, of which are two types: (1) D-RAM chips (dynamic random access memory), where one stores, retrieves, and restores information, and (2) ROM chips (read only memory), chips that contain information that is always the same (e.g., two plus two is always equal to four). The next basic type are called the microprocessors—these perform the calculations. Lastly, there are logic chips that direct the computer's activities.

Chips generally come in several commercial varieties as well, divided not by function but by source. There are proprietary chips that are sold to many customers but are made by only one chip manufacturer. The microprocessors made by Intel are mostly of this variety. There are commodity chips, chips that are interchangeable, made by a variety of vendors who compete with each other on a price basis. Most D-RAM chips are of this type. And there are custom chips. These are designed and manufactured to specifications incorporating proprietary logic. Some computer companies such as IBM make their own proprietary chips.

Over the past few decades, chips have progressively gotten faster and contain more and more circuits. This is extremely important because it has brought us to a departure point in terms of discussing data processing in the 90s.

One doesn't have to understand how computers work to grasp why putting more logic circuits on a chip is important. It requires a very rudimentary understanding of the principles of physics. The following is the kindergarten explanation.

First, here are two things you need to know: (1) Electricity is nothing more than a flow of electrons; (2) electrons move at a very fast rate but slower than light.

A computer works as follows: A set of chips called the central processor, sends out instructions in pulses of electrons. These instructions require information to be retrieved from the memory, transported to the central processing unit (CPU), and have some calculation done with them. Then the original data, plus the result, are stored back in the memory. As computers speak in binary (only ones and zeros), just to construct a simple four-digit number (in decimal terms) in binary requires a great deal of fetching from the memory. Fortunately, computers do this type work so fast that it seems relatively easy. Nevertheless, the number of instructions required merely to add 9852 and 6841 is substantial. To accomplish this simple math those electrons have to go marching around the computer retrieving from memory, processing, and putting the data back. The electrons can only move so fast, at some rate slower than the speed of light. Consequently, the further they have to go to get a piece of information and bring it back to the central processor, process it, and re-store it, the slower the whole operation is going to be.

The speed of performing one set of instructions is called "clock time" and is measured in nanoseconds (billionths of a second). A very fast clock time would be, for example, two nanoseconds. This means that a set of operations would be performed in two billionths of a second. Computers operate in a burst mode called "synchronous." A series of operations occur in one burst, then there is a pause, then the next series. When a burst occurs, it requires the electrons to physically make the trip. This brings us to a key point. The closer the circuits are together, the less distance the electrons have to go and the faster the computer can run, all other things being equal.

Moreover, we can think of semiconductor circuits as minute buckets that contain electricity rather than water. When a circuit's state is changed, the bucket is emptied or refilled. The closer they are, the quicker this process can occur.

Obviously then, the more circuits you can put on a tiny chip, the better. It's far better to put more circuits on a chip than to have lots and lots of chips on a PC board, because the circuits can then be microns (millionths of an inch) as opposed to inches apart). Also, it accelerates emptying and filling the buckets.

The speed of computers increases exponentially with the closeness of the circuits. Seymour Cray, one of the pioneers of the supercomputer and probably the most brilliant of the supercomputer developers is a man who believes passionately in circuit density. Circuit density creates tremendous heat if it is extreme. The more advanced supercomputers are literally encased in ultra-cool liquids to bleed off the heat that is generated by the speed of the circuits.

Nevertheless, even for smaller computers, having greater circuit integration was the key to vastly expanded speeds as well as a reduction in required electrical usage. More has happened in the last 5 years to accelerate the speed of computing than in the previous 10 years. In the mid-80s the manufacturing of semiconductor devices (chips) became essentially stabilized. The Japanese refined the concept of statistical process control (we pioneered it). By using statistical process control, they were able to make the manufacturing of semiconductor devices far more stable than it had been in the past. As a result, much higher yields (good chips versus ruined chips) became possible. This had two effects. First, it permitted significantly larger chips, created tighter geometries. Second, it radically reduced manufacturing costs, allowing the Japanese to gain the lead in high-volume chips.

The number of transistors (circuits) packaged on a single chip has been rapidly increasing. If the trend continues, according to Intel Corporation, devices with up to 50 million transistors will be manufactured by the year 2000. This compares to 1.5 million now and only 50,000 in 1980. This massive increase in the number of transistors per chip has created and will continue to create tremendous increases in raw power.

In the mid-80s a typical departmental-sized minicomputer, which would require full air-conditioning and a small dedicated, room, had the capability of doing less than one to two MIPs. A MIP is the most basic measure of raw processing power; it stands for millions of instructions per second, meaning the computer can issue commands at that rate. By contrast, IBM just introduced a workstation (a computer that simply sits on a desk) with 27 MIPs of power, approximately a 30 times increase in the last 5 years.

These devices are not entirely comparable; the minicomputer can do some things that the IBM workstation cannot, but the workstation has much more raw processing power. The fact that a vast amount of processing power can be put in a small box on a desk has removed a significant percentage of the data processing function from the data processing department and put it in the hands of the executive or engineer himself. This has already had significant side effects in the way in which businesses are operated. Large amounts of information are now available, in a relatively user-friendly way, to white-collar employees of all kinds. Also, our national engineering capability has been greatly increased by this power, as has our manufacturing efficiency. The ability to do "just-in-time" inventory control is one example.

As applications have become more user friendly—less specialized knowledge is required to use them—demands on the processing power have increased geometrically. Consequently, most of the increases in power have been absorbed by making computers smaller and easier to use. This has made them accessible to people who could not use them before.

A wide variety of new computer applications are going to be available during the decade, because of the great incremental increases in computing power. According to Intel, a significant quantity of processing power is going to be allocated to human interface. Some of the newer forms of human interface are very primitive at present but will mature over the decade. These are: voice generation, voice recognition, image recognition, handwriting recognition, motion video, and advanced multitasking.

An important development will be increased interface with CD ROM (similar to a CD player), which means having enormous amounts of retrievable data on a laser disk. A CD ROM has huge random access storage capabilities and also the potential to integrate video and audio imaging.

Another big step will be advanced-generation languages that will be so user friendly that a user will be able to give the computer commands in English rather than in programming commands. In subsequent chapters we will discuss some of the developments we see emerging and some of the companies we see taking advantage of those trends.

One place in which those trends are going to emerge is in microchip technology; chip-making techniques continue to evolve rapidly. This evolution will continue to pit American chip manufacturers and large users of semiconductors such as IBM and AT&T against Japanese companies. Microchip manufacturers are increasingly using ultraviolet light; also companies may begin to use X rays and electron beams for production to make much smaller geometries. Currently sophisticated microprocessors can have 1.5 million transistors and the lines that separate them can be less than one micron in width (which is approximately 100th of the width of a human hair). To repeat, one of Intel's goals is to develop chips with over 50 million transistors.

Presently, technology for chip etching involves the use of light to pattern the wafer. Conventional light, however, has a wave length too large to resolve very fine lines and consequently there are experiments taking place with X rays to etch the silicon in much smaller geometries. X rays could also improve yields because they penetrate dust. Chips having vastly increased numbers of transistors would have to have much closer geometries, perhaps as close as .02 microns.

As we have noted previously, having more transistors on a chip makes computers faster by an exponential factor. Faster speeds enable the computers to be smaller and cheaper in relation to their power. Also, faster speeds allow the computer to process much more sophisticated software that in turn will allow much more advanced functions or make simple functions more easy to use.

From all of this a variety of fast-growing companies will emerge during the decade. Some may not even exist now. Many will probably be found in three main areas, semiconductor technology, small computer technology, and software.

CHAPTER 12

SEMICONDUCTORS—THE BASIC BUILDING BLOCK

As children, we were always taught that the exception makes the rule. It is almost always true that one of the best places to find growth stocks is to look for companies with high unit volume growth; in other words, companies that are selling more product every year. It is also true that an investor should try to find companies involved with industries that are growing rapidly. By following these rules an investor would conclude that semiconductor manufacturers probably should be the best growth stocks available. They are, however, treacherous investments, although occasionally spectacular stocks can be found in the group.

Semiconductor companies are obviously supplying the building blocks of the data processing industry; to the extent that they are able to make their geometries tighter they will be the engine of most new developments, as was their role in the 1980s. It would be logical then to assume that the demand for these new, faster semiconductors would be very great on a worldwide basis, extremely important, and therefore represent a source of great stock market profit. I think it fair to say, however, that semiconductor stocks have caused as many broken hearts in the stock market as have any other group. Therefore, to some extent, chip makers are the exception that proves the rule.

The reason why this is true lies in the inherently contradictory nature of the business itself. As I have described to you, there are three basic kinds of chips: memory, logic, and microprocessors. There are, as well, various other kinds of chips, including the semicustom circuits and variants thereof. It is true that the worldwide demand for semiconductors is growing just as fast as one might think that it would. Data processing itself is growing on a worldwide basis at about 10 percent per year, significantly higher than most other industries. The demand for processing power also grows exponentially. The smaller and faster the computers are, the more they tend to be used. This increases the demand for power, and consequently, more semiconductors.

Furthermore, the movement of data processing out of the central location onto the desks of white-collar workers created a very rapid demand for semiconductor chips of all kinds. Moreover, semiconductor chips are used in a lot of applications that are not strictly data processing related; automobile makers are using progressively increasing quantities of microprocessors to control a variety of functions from ignitions to stereos. Home appliance manufacturers are using increased amounts of chips to provide electronic interfaces between the user and the machine itself. It is a paradox, therefore, that it is difficult to make money in semiconductors.

The reason why semiconductor stocks are so difficult is: despite the unit volume demand increasing at a very rapid rate for all forms of chips, the manufacturing capacity has increased faster than demand on a global basis. As a consequence, the prices of semiconductor circuits have dropped as fast, and in some cases faster, than the demand for them has risen. Consequently, the dollar volume that is normally runs parallel to a high level of unit volume growth, has shown an erratic growth pattern.

The most price-vulnerable type of chip has been the D-RAM chip. D-RAM chip unit volume has grown very rapidly as computer memories have grown geometrically in capacity. However, on a per circuit or per bit basis, prices have plunged. This is because the Japanese have been able to standardize and improve upon the quality control techniques used in semiconductor manufacture, especially in high volume, low-value-added chips such as D-RAMs. Therefore, capacity overseas has risen so dramatically that it has hurt American manufacturers of D-RAMs. In America, very few manufacturers still exist. This has not entirely been to the detriment of the American electronics industry. Purchasers of D-RAMs have been willing to allow the Japanese to dominate the production of D-RAMs so that the price would fall; this has been one of the factors that made computers progressively less expensive during the 80s.

Microprocessors are a somewhat different story. A microprocessor chip is much more expensive than a D-RAM because of the much more sophisticated nature of the product, the more difficult manufacturing and design process involved, and the smaller production runs. In the United States, two companies have dominated the manufacturing of merchant microprocessor chips. The first is Intel; the second, Motorola. Intel remains one of the leaders in the semiconductor industry, either domestic or foreign. A company with extraordinarily good technology, it has been able to dominate a fairly substantial part of the microprocessor world. This has permitted it to introduce a series of faster and faster products that have, in turn, enabled the company to generate spurts of excellent earnings growth. Intel should definitely be considered a growth stock for the 90s. Its latest microprocessor, the 486, is being incorporated into a variety of fast, smaller computers and we believe that Intel is one of the few semiconductor companies that definitely has the capability to stay on the forefront of technological excellence.

It is important to note that even Intel goes through periods where its profitability growth can lag. These are usually followed by periods where its profitability once again accelerates. This is the nature of the semiconductor industry itself, which is characterized by boom and bust cycles, because periods of overcapacity develop due to excess inventory followed by periods of undercapacity characterized by hoarding. Consequently, we refer to Intel as a cyclical growth company; a company that does not grow every year but, over time, has the potential to grow rapidly.

There is a cliché in the semiconductor industry sometimes called "Moore's law." (It is only a law in the sense that Murphy's law is a law.) Moore's law dictates that density increases by the factor of 2 about every 18 months. This implies that there will be very substantial increases in the number of transistors on a semiconductor by the end of the decade. As we have noted, Intel will probably be one of the primary creators and beneficiaries of this trend.

The total semiconductor industry revenue is approximately $45 billion. In the past it grew at a compound rate 15 percent. However, as we have noted, it is very cyclical. There have been periods where it has grown not at all: 1985 to 1986 and then 1987 to 1988 were periods where the growth was limited. 1989 had some growth, as did 1990. The current year is uncertain. As always, unit prices are coming down.

There are some important considerations concerning the nature of the semiconductor business during the decade that an investor must watch. First, there are some significant questions about the nature of computer architecture. One company that has dedicated its business to one side of this argument is MIPS Computer Systems, Inc. This is a very rapidly growing designer of RISC/UNIX processors. (They do not do the manufacturing themselves, which has both advantages and disadvantages for the 1990s). It is a stock to watch, however. We will go into this in greater detail in subsequent chapters, but whether UNIX develops into the dominant operating system or not will determine whether this company becomes a major factor in the industry. Secondly, other architectural questions which we will discuss (RISC versus CISC) will be important. The face of the semiconductor industry could be dramatically altered by the outcome of the debates. The coming turf battle between workstations and PCs will also be a big factor in determining the Intel's success after mid-decade.

One of the big developments of the 1980s was the emergence of custom-designed chips that are application-specific and proprietary. Application-specific integrated circuits (ASICs) are chips that are produced for only one machine; they are designed for only one application and are manufactured either by the design company or by another company. Several companies were pioneers in developing ASICs. The principal domestic pioneer was LSI Logic. In Japan, Fujitsu seems to dominate this type of business. It should be noted, however, that Intel also designs and produces ASICs.

There have been two divergent trends even within this business. The first has been toward purely custom-designed chips. This requires the designer to create specific circuits to fulfill the desired function. The second has been the use of standard cells that are predesigned logic circuits that can be assembled in a certain way to create large units of function.

ASIC designers never attained the level of profitability that they might have. Often, one company designed a circuit only to find that the client would have it mass-produced overseas, thus losing the manufacturing leverage. However, ASICs set the stage for a new type of device that could be very important in the 90s, programmable logic devices (PLD).

The programmable devices are created in silicon, like normal chips, but are then programmed by the use of decoupling or coupling fuses within the circuits themselves, such that an off-the-shelf chip can be customized electronically to perform the functions that the computer designer wishes to have it perform. In this interesting new approach PLDs have the advantages of ASICs in that they are custom, application-specific, and proprietary. However, they are superior to ASICs in that they require much less design and set-up time to create a new chip. They can be debugged quickly and efficiently, and upgrades can be made much more quickly. There are three small PLD companies that may be interesting stocks; they are growing very rapidly at present. They are Altera, Xilinx, and Lattice. They all use slightly different techniques. Altera and Xilinx are high-end producers. Lattice produces less complex circuits. These companies have the advantage that they are doing it "FABless" (FABS are large manufacturing plants).

Essentially they all subcontract out the manufacturing of these chips, which gives them business characteristics substantially more like software producers than traditional semiconductor fabricators.

FABS, the industry jargon for semiconductor plants, are becoming extraordinarily expensive and the need for tighter geometries requires more and more sophisticated equipment including clean-rooms. The amount of money required to build a FAB is increasing at such a rate that smaller companies cannot actually produce their own semiconductors. But because the FABless companies do not have this capital commitment, they have high returns on their assets. It remains to be seen, however, whether these companies can, in the long run, continue to be as profitable while relying on other companies. It is possible that as fabrication has become more expensive, FABS will command a higher price, possibly driving FABless companies into extinction. It is for this reason that they are known as "lite" semiconductor companies, a name derived from the beer, rather than any light-sensitive processing technique. At present, however, and for the next several years, there is significant capacity worldwide and the FABless companies can grow rapidly if they have the right products.

As we have discussed, geometries will get tighter in the 1990s. This will require more expensive plants and, consequently, improvements in manufacturing techniques will have to be made to progress toward the 50–100 million transistor-per-chip goal.

It might help, at this point, to describe how an integrated circuit works and is manufactured so that a potential investor will have some understanding of companies that I refer to and of other semiconductor equipment companies as they come along. Again, this explanation is the kindergarden version.

An integrated circuit, or semiconductor, works because it has minute circuits etched on a substrate wafer of silicon. Silicon is a crystalline semi-conductor material with extremely controllable physical properties allowing it to conduct electricity in a very precise and ordered way. Imposed upon the silicon are various layers of other materials. These materials can be layered one on top of another. However, the more layers there are, the more sophisticated the chip, and the more expensive and difficult it is to make.

When electricity passes through the chip a field is created across individual circuits that enables electrical current either to pass or not pass into any specific circuit. If that circuit has a charge it represents one kind of electronic situation, or state; a lack of charge represents another state. Usually, these two different amounts of voltage in the circuit can be understood as representing ON or OFF.

A computer reads every one of its circuits and determines whether there is or is not voltage present in the circuit. It is thereby able to assign a value to that voltage. Positive voltage means ON, or the number one; less strong voltage means OFF, or the number zero. Since computers think in binary and compose all numbers out of ones and zeros, it is able to compose long strings of numbers from the presence or absence of voltage in a series of circuits.

The semiconductor circuits are created by placing some type of material impurities on the silicon. There are numerous kinds of materials, such as insulators, that can be placed in or on the silicon to create circuits and there are many different techniques for placing these materials. The impurities are then built up in layers, creating a three-dimensional matrix of circuits on the silicon.

Integrated circuits are designed as follows: First, the engineers design the chip, using powerful computers that create drawings of the circuit. These designs are very similar to architectural blueprints. The blueprints are then formed into what are known as masks. It should be noted that the mask covers not only the specific semiconductor chip, but the entire wafer from which many chips are made. Wafers are typically six inches in diameter and made out of very pure silicon. IBM and others have now gone to eight-inch wafers, which was considered an extremely difficult step because it was hard to purify silicon beyond the six-inch level. IBM is experimenting with 12-inch wafers in one location, which would have been considered unlikely if not impossible 10 years ago.

The mask is then placed in a machine that focuses light through it onto the wafer; the mask itself is a photosensitive material when exposed to light. The optics of these systems are dominated by Japanese companies, Nikon and Canon being leaders. Photo-resist is placed on the silicon and as the light passes through the mask the pattern is transferred to the silicon wafer. This is called ''scanning the wafer''—the light beam shines through the mask at different angles to expose more of the wafer. Another technique is called "stepping" and it involves moving the wafer in small increments to expose it progressively. Stepping and scanning both have advantages; an interesting company called Silicon Valley Group, which acquired the business of Perkin-Elmer, has developed a combination step and scan device that may be about to be accepted by IBM to process eight-inch wafers. If this happens, and it remains to be seen how effective it will be, the device could present an exciting growth stock for the early 1990s.

After the wafer is exposed to light, it is etched by photochemical process along the lines indicated on the mask. Several different approaches are then taken, depending on which metal is supposed to be either implanted or deposed on the silicon substrate. Once the process is complete, the wafer is then sliced-up into chips and then wire-bonded. The slicing, which is known as scribing, is generally accomplished with a diamond saw.

The individual chips then must be wire-bonded into packages. This means that the individual connections, all around the chip must be made into the little packages that contain the chips and these, in turn, must be connected by pins. A small company called Kulicke & Soffa has a product called ultrasonic bonding that is extremely interesting; this company may prove to be a good investment in the 1990s.

The key to any semiconductor company's future in the 1990s depends a lot upon the direction that computer architecture is going to take. Several different trends emerged in the late 1980s and are now converging upon one another. These trends will be discussed in the next few chapters. How these trends are resolved will determine, in large part, the direction of the semiconductor industry for the decade to come. For this reason, it is hard to speculate now on which companies will become potentially interesting investments. However, as more is known about the shape of the computer industry, more educated guesses can probably be made. Thus, while there are not many stocks, except Intel, that look like they have a competitive advantage in the 1990s, it is important to note that there may be some substantial developments in the semiconductor business forthcoming within the next five years. Investors should keep close contact with these trends by watching reports from technology-oriented brokerage firms. Reading the trade press can be helpful in generally maintaining a high level of scrutiny of this industry. Without doubt, there will be two or three important investments that will emerge as this industry evolves over the course of the decade. The ones I have mentioned all deserve watching, but are by no means sure things at present.

One small company does appear to have a proprietary fast-growing niche. This company, International Rectifier, produces a semiconductor chip called Power MOSFETs (it stands for metal-oxide-semiconductor-field-effect-transistor). This product is not designed for data processing but for a multitude of everyday products where power has to be regulated in small increments, as in intermittent windshield wipers. International Rectifier has just gotten patent rights to this product, which has reduced pricing pressure from bigger competitors, such as Motorola, and make it a rapidly growing profitable company. As MOSFET demand is growing 15 percent per year and since International Rectifier can control pricing, the company's financial characteristics will be much more favorable than most companies in the industry.

KEY INVESTMENT POINTS

1. Semiconductor companies have very high unit volume growth as the demand for computer power grows exponentially every year. However, the prices for chips drops consistently and this causes substantial variability in revenue growth patterns. As a result, most of these stocks are not classical growth stocks.

2. These companies' results are frequently influenced by the overall business cycle.

3. Investors frequently accord these companies high P/Es. Usually, this is after several years of growth. When the growth ends, multiples can contract significantly, causing sharp drops in the stocks.

4. The industry publishes a monthly ''book-to-bill'' ratio. This measures orders versus sales. A number above 1 is considered good, below 1, bad. Frequently the stocks react to this number.

5. At the peak of demand cycles, there is usually double ordering and shortages. This always makes investors euphoric. Beware, it never lasts. At the bottom of the cycle many companies slash prices of their chips and lose money; this doesn't last either. A contrarian approach sometimes works well, but only at the extremes.

6. The Japanese companies are very important factors in the business. They frequently emphasize share of market at the expense of profit.

7. Generally inexperienced investors should confine themselves to companies with new technology, preferably "FABless" ones. They can grow much faster and are less cyclical.

8. Few stock groups can cause as much indigestion.

CHAPTER 13

WORKSTATIONS AND PERSONAL COMPUTERS

The 1980s was an extremely significant decade for the development of computing. As we noted in the preceding chapters, a major evolution occurred during this period as the power of small computers matched and then exceeded minicomputers and even some low-end mainframes. This shifted the burden of computing onto the white-collar worker.

Part of the process was the development of software that permitted nontechnical people to interact with computers. There were two types of computers that evolved in parallel in the 1980s: workstations and personal computers; this evolution ran parallel until probably 1988 and then began to converge at a rapid rate. This convergence forms the basis for the growth of this industry in the 1990s, a growth that we feel will be spectacular, albeit somewhat unpredictable.

Workstations were probably commercially pioneered by Apollo Computer (now part of Hewlett-Packard) in the early 1980s. Somewhat later, Sun Microsystems, Inc., developed into a full line workstation company and thrust its way to the forefront of this extremely rapidly growing industry. Sun was established in 1981 and is now a multibillion dollar company. It was developed from work done at Stanford University; indeed, the name Sun is actually an acronym for Stanford University Network. Most of the seminal work in workstations occurred in Northern California at Stanford and Berkeley.

Workstations are nothing more than extremely powerful small computers. Like other small computers they can sit on a desk, yet they have extraordinary processing power, extremely high resolution graphics in many cases, and very sophisticated software. Until the last few years they have been exclusively commercially oriented toward engineering and scientific markets.

The emergence of workstations became possible because of the development of 32-bit microprocessors in the early 1980s. Microprocessors, as we have discussed, are the calculator chips of a computer. The number of bits a microprocessor can handle is extremely important. Think of a microprocessor as the stomach of a computer; its job is to digest food as fast as possible. The size of the mouth regulates whether it can eat in big chunks or little nibbles. A big chunk is 32 bits, a medium bite is 16 bits and a little nibble is 8 bits. A ''bit'' for those who do not know, is one binary digit. (Another term, *byte*, refers to a string of 8 bits and should not be confused with the term *bit* itself; memory space is quoted in bytes). As we have discussed, computers store information in memory. Obviously, since a computer only speaks in binary, the number 18 instead of requiring two digits requires many more. Consequently, a number of circuits are required to store the number 18. However, each unit of storage has to have an address, so the computer can know exactly where to get the information. The address is tagged onto the piece of information itself. The longer the string of bits that the computer can handle in one piece (the chunk in our analogy), the more of that string can be devoted to an address and the longer an address can be. This causes the available discrete addresses to grow exponentially in the same way that a seven-digit phone number system can handle vastly more homes than a five-digit one; there are more permutations. A 32-bit microprocessor handles information in strings of 32 bits at a time. As a consequence, the available addresses are much larger than with a 16-bit microprocessor and thus it works faster. Until the advent of workstations, small computers worked in 8- or 16-bit mode, sometimes in a combination of the two. Consequently, the advent of the 32-bit microprocessors made workstations much more powerful.

As a result, workstations began to work on problems that had been the domain of traditional computers. The early Apollo workstations had a number of features that were associated with large computers, including multitasking and relational data bases.

A relational data base is one that does not have to be defined in advance. New data related to a data base in existence can be added without rewriting the structure of the data base. In other words, if one had a data base relating to a company's employees and suddenly it became important to know the eye color of each worker, this fact can be added to the data base without rewriting the entire program. For large data base applications, this is a very advanced feature and an extremely important one for many businesses.

Another advance occurred in the operating systems. The operating system tells the computer how to work. Sun made the jump to the operating system UNIX, which had some distinct benefits, especially for scientific applications. UNIX is an operating system that has existed for a number of years. It was developed originally by AT&T and is being considered as a potentially universal operating system. It has some advantages over other operating systems by including a "virtual operating system and has an easy multitasking facility. "Virtual operating system" means that the computer constantly stores and retrieves information (swaps) from its internal memory onto its disk drive, which greatly enhances the capability of the computer. The easy multitasking capability means that the computer can do more than one thing at a time, giving it much greater flexibility.

Additionally, UNIX is portable, which means that applications written for UNIX can be transferred to other computers. By contrast, IBM uses proprietary operating systems, as does Digital Equipment Corp. for its mainframes. Applications cannot be easily transferred. Also UNIX is scalable: programs written on small computers can be transferred to large computers. UNIX does have some disadvantages. It is difficult to program and since it has a number of different versions slightly specific to each company, it does not have total universality. However, UNIX is an operating system that is extremely good for scientific applications and consequently it was a factor in making Sun the dominant workstation company.

The development that more than any other propelled Sun to the forefront was RISC architecture. Sun did not invent RISC; others such as Hewlett-Packard had been working on a commercial version for several years when Sun burst onto the scene. However, Sun was the first company to exploit RISC's commercial potential.

RISC is an acronym for reduced instruction set computing; it was developed to take advantage of a disparity between central processing and memory speed. The central processor refers to the combined calculation and logic function of the computer; it incorporates several microprocessor chips. As computers became more complex in the 70s and early 80s, the number of instructions a central processor had to issue to accomplish a task rose severalfold. Computer memories also became faster as D-RAM chips took geometric leaps in size. Consequently, by the early 80s most computers' memories were sitting around idle waiting for central processors to issue all their instructions. Sun capitalized on this by creating an architecture that used a much simplified set of instructions, hence RISC. The combination of 32-bit design, the UNIX operating system, and RISC architecture made Sun workstations blazingly fast for any computer, much less a small computer. The engineering community overwhelmingly adopted Sun workstations to do design, modeling, and graphics because its speed could handle these computation-intensive tasks.

Curiously, the newest central processors are now capable of such high speeds that now it is the memories that are no longer able to keep pace. We are in the process of moving from one-megabyte ($= 1$ million bytes, or 8 million bits) memory chips to four-megabyte memory chips. The one-megabyte can function at a clock speed of 80 nanoseconds, whereas the four-megabyte can function at a clock speed of 50 nanoseconds. While this is obviously an improvement, it in no way mirrors the improvement in speed of the newer central processing units. Consequently, some computers are verging on a condition where the CPU has to sit around doing nothing while the memory tries to keep up. This may introduce a whole new trend, the return to CISC (pronounced to rhyme with RISC). CISC stands for complex instruction set computing, which is essentially the way things were prior to Sun's popularizing of RISC.

As noted, one of the most amazing features of today's workstations is the incredible speed at which they work. Suddenly, in 1990, IBM has emerged as a technology leader in workstations. While Sun is still the largest factor, followed by Hewlett-Packard and DEC, IBM's share is rising fast.

To understand what IBM has achieved, it is important to understand a certain basic characteristic of computing. Computers work in synchronous mode; a burst of activity occurs, the computer pauses to test the states of all the chips, there is a period of inactivity, then another burst of activity occurs while new instructions are sent out. The number of bursts that can be sent out is called the clock speed and it is typically measured in nanoseconds (one billionth of a second). The fastest supercomputers function at a rate of two nanoseconds. It is generally true that most computers send one burst of instructions per clock cycle; this, intuitively, makes sense. IBM, however, has introduced a new workstation that works on a "super-scaler" principle that means it sends out more than one burst of instructions per clock cycle. (I confess that I don't understand exactly how this is done and I probably couldn't explain it even if I did.) Needless to say, however, it accelerates the processing power of the computer very substantially. As we have said, clock time relates in part to the density of the circuits, the nature of the architecture (RISC/SISC) and other matters.

The ability of IBM to incorporate more than one set of instructions per pulse has a potential to greatly accelerate the processing power of a computer without making the circuits denser.

How far IBM can go with this trend, is at present, unclear, but it does open processing horizons for workstations. This new workstation, the 6600 is ultra-fast. By way of example, let us compare this new workstation with an IBM 370, which was the mainstay of the IBM mainframe product line of the 1970s. A 370 model 168 operated at about 2 MIPS (millions of instructions per second) and would have cost $4 million in 1970 dollars. It would have had 2 megabytes of internal memory (RAM) and typically a minimum of 400 megabytes of external storage. By contrast, the IBM 6600, the new super-scaler workstation, can go as high as 41 MIPS and soon will be able to achieve 50 to 80 MIPS. It has 10 megabytes of internal memory (RAM) and the same 400 megabytes of external storage. Instead of the $4 million that the 370 cost, it would probably cost (these numbers are rough and depend on configuration) around $40,000.

The drop in direct cost is extraordinary! The workstation is 100 times less expensive and gives much greater processing power. Moreover, the indirect costs are immeasurably smaller. An IBM 370 would require an entire room, which would of course have to be air-conditioned, and as 370s were water-cooled, it would have to have a source of fresh water. Also it would have to be maintained in a very clean, static-free environment and would require perhaps several technicians to operate it. By contrast, the IBM 6600 can sit on a desk and function in normal office temperatures. It can be used directly by an engineer or businessman and requires no sophisticated, specially trained personnel. Consequently, the indirect cost in terms of salaries and office real estate is dramatically reduced.

While the cost is far smaller, the throughput is much higher. These workstations can do a variety of very sophisticated tasks including solids modeling, which require the very high processing speeds formerly only available on extremely sophisticated super computers. More importantly, workstations can now be configured into networks which distribute the processing load among the computers. A network of workstations can now be as powerful as a distributed data processing network using a variety of terminals and mainframes. Thus, in the computing world of the mid to late 90s the mainframe may disappear except for the very largest applications. New networking configurations have, in essence, overcome some of the input/output/multitasking problems associated with smaller localized computers. In other words, workstations can now accomplish a great deal of what much larger computers could formerly accomplish and, as a result, the data processing load is being rapidly shifted out of a centralized point to distributed systems.

While a fair amount of engineering and technical functions are now accomplished on very powerful workstations, there is substantial growth left in that market. Engineering is one of those markets which requires progressively more sophisticated hardware and software as each generation develops cost-effective solutions. Cost effective means more and better designs accomplished by fewer engineers. Consequently, we see the growth of the workstation business continuing to be very rapid.

One of the major questions for the 1990s however, is to what extent workstations will take over business-related applications. To answer to this question, we have to first examine the other parallel stream, personal computers (PCs). The other stream began in 1977 with the introduction of the Apple II and the Tandy TRS80. These were the first two personal computers to achieve high volume sales. Unlike workstations, they were designed for a purely personal use and had comparatively small processing power. They were eight-bit computers, had limited software, and were comparatively inexpensive.

In 1981, IBM introduced its PC, which was a 16-bit machine, somewhat larger. This became very successful among businessmen due to the introduction of one of the great computer programming successes of all time, Lotus 1-2-3. Lotus, which provided a spreadsheet format that was powerful and easy to use, had almost universal appeal to individuals and businessmen; its availability created a boom in the personal computer market. Lotus actually was a follow-up product to another PC-based spreadsheet, known as Visicalc, but Lotus 1-2-3 had greater simplicity and more features. Most people could learn how to use Lotus in a matter of hours rather than days.

Coupled with accelerating capability of most PCs, Lotus pushed the PC market into a very rapidly growing state. IBM contributed to this by having the foresight to open its architecture to anyone who wished to write software. Consequently, hundreds of programmers developed products for the IBM PC, which greatly accelerated its acceptance.

The IBM PC itself represented a departure from IBM's normal practice which emphasized total integration. The PC was manufactured out of standard components, including the Intel microprocessor. Consequently, IBM made its product vulnerable to an army of competitors who essentially reproduced the same computer. Rather than making IBM unsuccessful, this made it more successful because the larger population of IBM-like computers engendered even more software.

The PC revolution developed very rapidly during the early 1980s. By 1986, Intel had developed its first 32-based microprocessor, the 386. Memory capacity had already expanded from a fourth of a megabyte to several megabytes. In the mid-80s the availability of hard disk drives provided substantially greater off-line storage than had previously been available. Prior to hard disk drives, most information was stored on floppy disks which were slow, cumbersome to use, vulnerable to disk error and easy to lose. The hard drive replaced floppies, permitting initially 10 megabytes of memory to be stored. Now 1700 is possible and the number continues to grow.

Compaq was one of the companies that capitalized on these trends. (We mentioned Compaq previously as an example of a great 1980s growth stock.) Compaq's original business was copying the IBM PC product line; soon it began to improve on it. Among the improvements that are associated with Compaq, was the development of portable computers and finally, in the late 1980s, laptops—which are no larger than an old portable typewriter (indeed smaller than some). Laptops are generally regarded as being in the 12–17 lb. range. However, Compaq has recently introduced a notebook that weighs 6–8 lbs. Many companies have followed suit; a newer development is the palmtop which weighs 1–2 lbs. These have limited utility because their keyboards are too small. Hewlett-Packard just announced a checkbook-sized computer with spreadsheet capability. It is unclear how successful this will be.

Of all the developments in PCs, few things were as important as the introduction, in 1986, of the graphical user interface (GUI), initially pioneered in the Apple Macintosh. I use the term *pioneered* advisedly because there is significant litigation as to the proprietary nature of some of these GUI technologies. A great deal was actually developed by Xerox in their research facility in Palo Alto for a computer (which never actually gained much commercial success) known as the Star. These technologies however, were left unprotected, and Steve Jobs, the very brilliant founder of Apple Computer, saw in them the promise of a major move forward in PC computing.

GUIs are a variety of techniques of screen presentation and commands that enable computers to be much more user friendly. Until recently, the Microsoft, Inc., operating system for small computers (MS/DOS), which has been dominant in the field, followed a format similar to other kinds of operating systems in that they required extensive use of manuals to learn how to operate them. MS/DOS provided character-user interface that required users to learn commands; for example, the screen always reverts to a simple prompt, which requires the user to perform some command that has to be looked up in the manual or memorized. In order to save a file in memory, retrieve a file, or do any of the other normal routine functions the commands had to be learned. While this is not an impossible task, it is cumbersome, especially for people who are not trained in computers.

Apple's graphical user interfaces, which came packaged with a new computer known as the Macintosh in 1986, provided the user with a variety of easy-to-use symbols (called "icons") on the screen, by which a nontechnical person could very rapidly develop proficiency with the computer without memorizing commands. Coupled with a device called a "mouse," which allows the user to move a cursor around the screen without touching the typewriter keyboard, GUIs made the computer easy to learn and use. This was extremely important for business because it enabled a company to train its personnel to use computers much more rapidly and with fewer problems. It spurred the commercial success of the Macintosh as a major product for Apple.

Apple has frequently referred to this ease-of-use capability in its advertising on TV. It has taken until recently for Microsoft, which dominates the basic software for small computers other than Apple, to counter with a similar program, called Windows 3.0. This has resulted in some litigation between the two companies, but nevertheless it underscores that increasing user friendliness is the future direction for business computing. I firmly believe by the end of the 1990s, icons will be replaced by direct verbal communication between the computer and the individual. By the mid-90s PCs will recognize and respond to handwritten commands and information.

Another development which was extremely important for the Macintosh and again caused a dramatic upsurge in computing was the development of desktop publishing. Prior to the 80s only professional printers had the ability to format a page of written text, using a variety of type fonts; to move sentences around on the page; and to include graphics with text.

In the 80s the ability to do these things on a PC was developed. It had enormous value to business for producing newsletters and marketing brochures. Desktop publishing as it became known, was made commercial by a software capability developed by Adobe Systems, as well as the development of the laser printer, which gave much clearer copies then had previously been available. The Adobe software, called Postscript became available on the Macintosh, making it the ideal desktop publishing machine. Postscript provided capability for changing type fonts. Pagemaker (another software package) permits electronic cutting and pasting for reformatting pages. A Macintosh with these two pieces of software and a laser printer can publish a magazine in small quantities. More recently, another little company, called Caere, has developed a product that allows a page of written text to be scanned into the memory of the Macintosh where it can then be reformatted on screen in a different print format. Caere has also gone a step further and has actually produced a hand scanner that can be used to scan the pages without putting them through a large piece of equipment.

By 1990, PCs have evolved to the point where they have very substantial business capabilities. The more rapid PCs have considerable power (17 MIPS), very advanced software, and a good deal of internal storage capacity. Also, there is a huge software library designed for every business, ranging from accounting to desktop publishing to spreadsheets. There is no doubt, however, that the workstation manufacturers such as Sun and the manufacturer of business-related PCs such as Apple and Compaq are on a collision course with each other. Sun has already announced that it will introduce workstations into the business environment, and as personal computers have become more powerful they have penetrated the low end of the engineering market, workstation's turf.

Workstations are presently much more powerful than PCs, but they are more expensive and do not have the abundance of business-related software that PCs do. There is also some question as to how much power is actually needed for business applications. The more powerful PCs can already process the largest business spreadsheets in a blink of an eye.

Nevertheless, workstations are encroaching significantly onto the minicomputer market. Recently, Sun revealed that 30 percent of its sales are to the commercial nontechnological market. The actual numbers of units are still modest. Sun is selling about 200,000 commercial workstations versus 2 million Macintosh and 20 million IBM-type PCs per year. The dollar value is more comparable, however, as the Sun average sales price is much higher. At present, business seems to like UNIX/RISC as a replacement for low end minicomputers and small mainframes in distributed networks. Whether the price of workstations drop enough so that the PC market becomes severely impacted, is another question. There is little doubt that workstations as a class will grow rapidly in the 90s but at whose expense is unclear.

In my opinion, the outcome will be determined by software. Eventually, software will become so complex that it will require very rapid processing speed. Moreover, although the software will be complex, it will be very easy to use; the direction of software is toward greater user friendliness. Software will also incorporate accelerated multitasking and multimedia applications. This will be made possible by the universality of CD/ROM, which will be standard storage by the mid-90s. An entire encyclopedia can be stored very easily on a CD/ROM disk and information can be retrieved in a random access way just as a music CD retrieves whatever song you want to hear without having to search through the entire record. The emergence of CD/ROM as an off-line storage medium for small business computers will make possible enormous advances in terms of graphics and displays. It will also consume a large amount of processing power and it is for this reason that the workstation manufacturers may ultimately overcome the conventional PC makers.

However, through the mid to early 90s, the PC makers will retain their share of the business market by virtually having more user-friendly software. Also, PC makers will provide smaller, more physically portable systems such as laptops, notebooks, and palmtops. These will have great utility with the advent of the digital cellular phones due in the mid-90s; it will permit an executive to tie into a network literally from anywhere.

The company which could benefit greatly from the trend toward smaller computers is Conner Peripheral, which dominates the world market for small disk drives. Conner has consistently been able to stay ahead of its competitors. Its standard drive is now only 3.5 inch in diameter and one inch tall. This little drive can hold 40 megabytes of memory. Recently Conner has moved to a 2.5 inch drive. Conner was one of the fastest-growing companies of the late 80s. It should continue to grow rapidly in the 90s as the proliferation of very small, very light computers continues.

Astride this question of workstation versus PC, with a foot firmly in each camp, is IBM. IBM now has surged to the technical forefront of the workstation market with the 6600 and is certainly the volume leader in the PC market as well. To add to the confusion, IBM just announced a joint venture with its old nemesis, Apple, to develop a future generation PC. This sent tremors through the industry and may undermine both Intel and Microsoft's position in the future. The ultimate outcome of this battle will be connected to other computer issues which are: networks of workstations versus mainframe computers, RISC versus CISC, UNIX versus all other operating systems. These are the main questions that are going to be faced by the industry over the next five years. The resolution will determine the nature of the small business computer market in the late 90s.

KEY INVESTMENT POINTS

1. Computers are getting smaller and small computers are getting more powerful. This is happening at a very fast rate. One result is that the line between PCs and workstations is getting blurred. Investors should know where on the continuum his target company's products fit. Reading trade magazines and talking to salespeople in computer stores can be of great help.

2. The final battle between RISC/UNIX and CISC/DOS-WINDOWS-OS2 has yet to be fought. The outcome will influence the price of many stocks in the industry. An investor should understand the nature of this battle. The IBM/Apple permutation is another competing axis to watch.

3. Both PC and workstation sales are growing rapidly but depend on frequent improvements in price/performance. To be successful, a company must stay on the forefront of this rapidly moving axis. On the other hand, beware of the large-scale product transition.

4. Despite overall rapid growth, PC and workstation companies are cyclically influenced and can be subject to poor earnings in bad economic times. In boom times, they are sometimes hurt by shortages of components. Both can result in very disappointing earnings growth for one or two quarters. This can drop a stock precipitously.

5. Beware the forecasts of management. As these companies often have very fast SG&A growth (see glossary), any shortfall in revenues often brings dramatic earnings drops.

6. An investor should think of these companies as fast ships with thin hulls. They can be great growth stocks, but change comes

very fast and the volatility can be extreme. Because of this volatility, P/E multiples are often lower than growth rates would warrant. Compaq is a good example; it has been a wonderful investment, despite never being accorded a high multiple. A potential investor should not be unduly seduced by an overly low multiple in these stocks however. This can be typical.

CHAPTER 14

SOFTWARE—THE ENGINE OF DATA PROCESSING GROWTH IN THE 1990s

Software development will determine the shape of the data processing industry in the 90s. The demand for data processing worldwide is growing inexorably. The fact that the industry has periodic slowdowns in its revenue growth does not obviate the fact that the basic demand for processing power is growing very rapidly; some forecasters say that demand for "MIPS," the basic unit of computing power, is growing at 25 percent per year. The slowdowns merely reflect the fact that the price of equipment does not keep up with their power, so the same dollar volume of sales can purchase significantly more power from one year to the next.

As noted in previous chapters, computers in the 90s will become exponentially more powerful than they were in the 80s. This trend has been in progress since computers first became commercial products (around 1945). An issue discussed in Chapter 13 was which type of small computer was going to dominate the latter half of the decade, workstations or PCs. Workstations, we noted, have become already extraordinarily powerful and this power will increase dramatically during the decade. Similarly, PCs have also become very powerful. The question is, how much will businesses pay for this increased power?

Engineers can always use more computer power. One of the rapidly developing areas of computer-aided design (CAD) is solids modeling. Creating a computerized model of a three-dimensional structure requires enormous processing capability, because, to make the model accurate, as many points as possible across the three-dimensional object have to be mathematically defined and recomputed. The ability to model solids and other three-dimensional phenomena such as thunderstorms, becomes increasingly more useful as the modeling becomes accurate. For example, it is possible through very fast, very powerful computers (such as Cray supercomputers) to test entire aircraft on a computer, as opposed to in a wind tunnel. This is because computers now have enough power to model air flows and other physical phenomena. The more dots that can be filled in on a three-dimensional model the more accurate it will be. Obviously, filling in these dots mathematically requires extremely fast processing speeds. Solids modeling is one way that engineers utilize the great advances in processing power.

The products of a small, very rapidly growing company, Alias Research, is another example. Alias provides software that harnesses the power of the new ultra-fast workstations. This software enables an industrial designer to design an object such as a perfume bottle, manipulate its image on a monitor, see how it looks in different colors, under different lighting, and from any angle. An object can be designed much more rapidly this way, and many companies are adopting this approach, including Honda. It replaces the expensive, time-consuming solid-model step and accelerates the introduction of new designs.

While there are a large number of engineers in the United States and overseas, only a fraction have powerful workstations on their desks. As a result, the market for workstations among engineers and architects is still growing and will continue to be a good market. Moreover, there is always the opportunity to sell better, more-advanced software to engineers that already have workstations.

In business applications, however, power does not necessarily translate into a higher level of revenue. Most business applications, except for the very large batch jobs, such as payroll, accounting, and data base manipulation, do not require tremendous processing speeds. There are admittedly some companies that require on-line computers, for example in airline reservation systems, automatic teller devices, and brokerage firm order-entry systems. These utilize a great deal of processing power. However, most executive, clerical, and staff applications, such as word processing, do not require either large internal memories, substantial disk storage, rapid communications, or ultra-fast processing speeds. A typical executive, using even the most advanced spreadsheets, such as Excel or the newer versions of Lotus 1-2-3, does not create spreadsheets of such enormous magnitude or complexity that they challenge the newer computers. As a result, the question arises whether subsequent generations of small computers can actually be sold to business at prices that reflect their expanded capability.

A computer is nothing more than a sophisticated machine tool. As a result, unless computers develop continuously increasing functionality, the computer industry will come to have the same kind of boom and bust characteristics that one finds among machine tool companies. When the economy is expanding, these businesses will do well; when the economy is contracting, sales will fall off dramatically. For computer sales to grow in all environments, each new model must provide much greater utility, or buyers will stick with the old.

Mainframes are already showing sensitivity to the economy. The bigger companies that primarily sell mainframes have not shown growth stock characteristics for several years. This would include IBM and Digital Equipment. Despite the fact that IBM has highly competitive products in the faster-growing areas of the market, such as workstations and more advanced PCs, it nevertheless derives a very significant portion of its sales from mainframes and associated software. Consequently, IBMs growth is extremely sluggish. Of course, it is hard to imagine any company with revenues as large as IBMs growing at an overly rapid rate; it is estimated that IBM will have sales of about $71 billion in the current fiscal year.

It is true that for the industry to sell larger quantities of small computers, they have to provide some reason for the purchaser to buy them. It is not sufficient for them simply to be faster, because existing computers are already fast enough to accomplish most business jobs with lightning speed. Consequently, the bridge to faster sales growth on the part of the data processing industry is software.

Software is a broad term covering everything from the operating systems that direct the computer's operations to specifically designed programming targeted toward single applications. Software has, generally speaking, lagged the development of hardware technologically. Hardware advances generally enable new software to be created. Until a new hardware system is produced, software writers cannot take advantage of the faster processing speeds that become available. Also, software design is much more labor-intensive and consequently takes longer to produce. This is the classical chicken/egg situation. In the 1990s, however, the development of new software will cause the data processing industry to continue to grow.

We have already discussed one of the aspects of software development; a number of computer companies, led in the workstation arena by Sun Microsystems, and in mainframes by Unisys, AT&T, and NCR, are trying to make UNIX the universal operating system. We have discussed the advantages this might confer. However, if such a universal operating system was adopted, it would radically change the nature of the computer industry. It is not surprising that IBM and Digital Equipment (DEC), while paying lip service to the virtues of UNIX, appear to be trying to slow down or stonewall its development. IBM and Digital Equipment each have their own proprietary operating systems that only work on their own computers. In fact, they have several different operating systems, depending on the category of computer; IBM has a different operating system for its mainframes than it does for its mid-sized computers, for example. IBM PCs use yet again other operating systems, designed principally by Microsoft.

The advantage to a manufacturer of having a proprietary operating system is that once a customer has equipment in his office, he may also invest in custom-developed software that only runs on the manufacturer's kind of equipment. Consequently, the customer becomes a captive. One aspect of having captive customers is that a vendor can frequently update their operating systems. In many cases this requires the customers to rewrite portions of their software at great expense. Also, there are frequently new semicustom applications which are produced en masse but come tailored for a specific machine and operating system. Once a customer has a substantial amount of software that runs on a proprietary operating system, it becomes impractical for him to switch to another hardware vendor.

IBM and DEC, which have large installed bases, are obviously reluctant to embrace an operating system that would permit software to run on just anybody's machine. If the entire world adopted the same type of UNIX, then the IBM-installed base could be replaced with computers from virtually anyone. This would cut IBM's price structure dramatically and also reduce the value of its installed base.

Companies having much smaller installed bases would prefer to have the world switch to UNIX. Whether or not the switch to UNIX occurs in the 90s is one of the big issues in the data processing industry in this decade. There are a number of vendors who would benefit from such a switch. Among them, Sun Microsystems, Pyramid, and MIPS, as well as the companies we have mentioned before. All of these have a vested interest in UNIX eventually displacing the proprietary operating systems. Such a development would be negative for many companies. Among them are Intel, Microsoft, DEC, and IBM.

While the battle over operating system architecture will continue in the 90s, I believe that the most important development of software will be extending ways in which individuals with no specific training can utilize the power of computers. As mentioned before, this will take many forms. In Chapter 13 we discussed graphical user interface (GUIs) and the importance they had on the development of Apple. I believe that a great deal more software of this type will be forthcoming in order to make the computer even more user friendly.

By the end of the decade, software will be available that totally eliminates a user's need to know most computer language. By mid-decade, communications with computers will be accomplished in near-English. One breakthrough in this regard is the ability of the computer to read handwriting. This is just emerging and will be expanded to universal use. The user will be provided with an electronic scratch pad on which he will write commands (which can be in the form of gestures, such as an ''x'' to delete) and make input in his own handwriting; the computer will be able to recognize the handwriting and follow the commands. Software to accomplish this will use a large amount of computing power as each handwritten letter will have to be interpreted and translated on a real-time basis into normal alpha-numeric characters (which of course are then translated into full numeric characters and ultimately into binary). Primitive versions of the handwriting entry system already exist and this should develop further through the decade. At the present such systems are confined to reading block letters; eventually cursive will be read as well. A small private company, Go-Corp. is introducing a notebook-sized computer that will use handwriting input. This product will probably be fairly primitive. Nevertheless, it is a major conceptual advance and useful in some applications such as field service or sales. In the future we will expect this modality to be an adjunct to bigger, desktop PCs rather than being discrete units. However, it will find many niche applications as well.

As I noted in Chapter 13, I believe that by mid-decade CD/ROM will be used in conjunction with small computers more than it currently is. In addition to providing a wealth of information on any conceivable subject, it will enable computers to retrieve video clips, pictures, and music. This will greatly enhance the interactive learning process associated with computers and will permit information to be given to the user in a much more enjoyable format.

Another probable development is that there will finally be commercially viable read and write CD players. Unlike CD/ROMs that simply contain information that has been encoded once and then can be accessed (such as an encyclopedia), read/write laser disks will allow the individual to use this device as storage. The storage capability in one of these units is much greater than conventional disk storage. Energy Conversion Devices has a license to Matsushita to provide such a device.

Ultimately, the keyboard will totally disappear. The computer, by mid-decade, will be able to understand verbally at least a limited selection of words. Eventually, a normal desktop computer will be able to understand words spoken at a normal pace. This will create a revolution in computing. And, from a clerical standpoint, Offices will change dramatically.

Already systems exist so that voice mail and electronic mail connect offices; individuals can leave typed messages on their computers that can be shipped to one or multiple locations with a touch of a button. The ability of a computer to recognize speech will allow a user to dictate a letter into a computer much as he would to his secretary, edit it verbally while watching the screen, and then dispatch it either to be displayed on someone's screen in a remote location or emerge in the form of a fax. As computers will also have voice synthesis chips of much improved quality, the computer might simply speak the message to the person who is to receive it. This would differ from a simple phone call in that the computer can be programmed to deliver the message at any time. The computer will then serve as a telephone and as an answering machine.

It is with the emergence of full voice recognition capability that the keyboard will totally disappear. This will finally permit computers to be useful even if they are only as large as calculators, because key pads (that are difficult to use when too small) will no longer be necessary.

Voice recognition will require very fast data processing speeds. The computer recognizes voices by breaking the many different oscillations that the human voice produces into digital intervals. The finer the intervals, the more accurately the computer can understand the sounds. Of course, full voice recognition will require the computer to understand a variety of sounds that are not language; they include pauses, exclamations, and background noise. The need for very fast processing speeds and large internal memory, simply to make the translation of the voice into a format that the computer can understand, will absorb a great deal of the increases in power that we see forthcoming, in the course of the decade.

Another form of software, that will absorb a great deal of processing power are more-advanced languages. These languages will permit individuals to issue commands to computers in a much more English-like format. Translating these commands into more rigid formats accepted by computers will require a great deal of processing power. Already, mainframe programming is so complicated that software has been devised to aid programming.

One very rapidly growing company now sells a form of software called "tools" in the industry, to help professional programmers program large computers. Knowledgeware Inc. is a company that helps organize and structure the programming function. This is needed because programming departments are being asked to write increasingly complex programs. Consequently, consistency is often lost and great inefficiency abounds. Knowledgeware software helps make programmers more efficient by bringing a level of organization and consistency to the job.

Another software company that helps mainframes function is BMC Software. This company's software enhances and improves the conventional software that runs on IBM mainframes. It works like a software turbocharger. IBM is far from being displeased; it encourages BMC because it helps mainframe sales. Both BMC and Knowledgeware are rapidly growing and deserve investor attention.

One of the developments that will affect the nature of data processing in the 90s is the diminishing usefulness of the small mainframe (sometimes known as "minicomputers"). While very large mainframes will doubtless still be used in business for large batch processes such as payroll and the storage and manipulation of large data bases, department-sized computing will be taken over by small computers connected in networks. This is already occurring at a rapid rate. Interconnecting workstations or PCs allows the processing load to be distributed among the various computers. These networks can also be connected to powerful storage devices, printers, and other forms of off-line equipment. Typically, a network will have one processor that will act as a traffic cop, called the "server" on the network.

One capability of a network is the ability to utilize processing power that resides on the network but is not being utilized. The ability of a network to divide tasks among a number of different processors gives the aggregate network tremendous capability. The newest concept is called "client serve computing." It relies on the server to do some preliminary calculations and then pass on the information to the "client," which is normally a PC or workstation on the network.

Since in any network the data is continuously shifted, networks require a lot of software to control the flow of data. Nevertheless, this can be an extremely cost-effective solution, as well as a flexible one, because it allows the network to rely to a lesser extent on any large processor.

Essentially, it replaces hardware with software; the software being used to control the network.

Today, most networks are joined together by what are known as LANs (local area networks). There are different kinds of LANs, some with greater capacity than others. Many LANs work by joining the computers together by coaxial cable, which has an extremely high level of data throughput. However, there is a technology that has been developed to tie together computers, using existing phone wiring. Two companies in particular have benefited from this approach, Synoptics and Cabletron Systems. I should mention that while this trend is growing rapidly it has not been undiscovered by the stock market; Cabletron was the best performing stock of 1990. Its approach uses devices known as intelligent hubs to tie together the hardware on the network. Hubs are controllers that usually fit inside the phone closet, permitting the phone network to act as a LAN and providing central network management.

The rapid proliferation of LANs has made one company, Novell, Inc., grow extremely rapidly. Novell designs and manufactures a high-performance LAN network operating system. This software, known as Netware, is installed in more than 500,000 LANs nationwide. More than 2,000 software developers have written applications for it. Because of this trend, Novell's revenues have increased from $3.8 million in 1983 to approximately $500 million in 1990. The stock has increased from about $1.50 at the end of 1984 to $34.00 last year. Novell is a prime example of how software is interacting with hardware to create the data processing solutions of the 90s.

Another company that is a prime beneficiary of the move to networking is Cisco. Cisco makes a product that is part hardware and part software that facilitates the next phase in the ongoing evolution of networking. Its product is known as a router. Routers are designed to tie more than one LAN together into a supernetwork. It permits a computer on one LAN to communicate directly with a computer on another LAN without sending messages to all parties. Consequently it is frequently the most efficient way of tying together multiple LANs. This business is in its infancy but is growing very rapidly.

A recent entry into the networking field is the very powerful Microsoft, Inc., which dominates many aspects of software for PCs. Their product will probably make slow progress against Novell. But as they themselves have said, they intend to "take the beach one grain of sand at a time." Microsoft recognizes the power inherent in marrying application software to networking software. This was almost accomplished by the merger of Lotus, manufacturer of the ubiquitous spreadsheet product Lotus 1-2-3 and Novell. The merger broke down over management issues but would have created a formidable company in PC software.

No chapter on software would be complete without a further discussion of Microsoft, Inc., one of the most extraordinary companies that has ever come onto the investing scene. In 1982 the company had net revenues of $24 million and a net income of $3 million. In the year ended June 1990, the company had sales of $1.1 billion and a net income of $279 million. Moreover, Microsoft has made W. H. Gates III, its founder, one of the richest men in America, a billionaire by his early thirties. If making money by one's own initiative, at an early age, were the only measure of a man's worth, then certainly Bill Gates, founder of Microsoft, would be head and shoulders above any other man in the world.

Microsoft derives its success from a combination of incredible aggressiveness, tremendous savvy, and a large portion of luck. The company develops a diverse line of systems and applications software for small computers, principally PCs. Early in the 80s the IBM and IBM-equivalent PCs standardized on an operating system developed by Microsoft, known as MS-DOS. As the number of PCs in the market expanded during the decade, Microsoft captured an enormous portion of the software business, as every computer has to have an operating system. Moreover, Microsoft was able to expand into application software, challenging Lotus with its spreadsheet entry, Excel. More recently, Microsoft has introduced a product called Windows 3.0, which provides enhanced graphical interface for MS-DOS.

In Chapter 13, we discussed the advantage that GUIs provided for Apple. Windows essentially allows MS-DOS to provide the same type of format for IBM, Compaq, and IBM-equivalents, partially nullifying Apple's advantage. This has resulted in some litigation between Apple and Microsoft. In the meantime, however, Windows 3.0 has been extraordinarily successful.

Microsoft also has developed a follow-up, more-advanced operating system called MS-OS/2. This operating system is designed to harness the capabilities of computers based on the Intel 80286 and 80386 microprocessors. It is presumed that the Intel 80486 will also work with OS/2. Microsoft appears to be moving to use Windows 3.0 as a bridge to either the OS/2 or the DOS environment. IBM is committed to the development of OS/2, which is very powerful but not yet commercially successful. The problem is an insufficient amount of application software has been written to make OS/2 fully desirable. Nevertheless, this is a relatively minor point. Whether the more powerful PCs of the future standardize on OS/2 or on a Windows-enhanced MS-DOS, Microsoft will still have the lion's share of the operating system market for the PCs of the 90s, unless the proposed IBM/Apple joint venture supplants it in the mid to late 90s.

Additionally, Microsoft has developed many microcomputer-language products, including Basic, Pascal, and C. It offers Xenix, which is a UNIX-based multiuser operating system. The future for Microsoft is nevertheless based upon the continued strength of the IBM PC/Intel format for small business computers.

In another camp, of course, is Sun Microsystem's UNIX/RISC workstations. If workstations begin to emerge as a dominant form of business computers in the late 90s, Microsoft's growth will doubtless be reduced. However, so many applications have now been written to work in conjunction with Microsoft's operating system that Microsoft will always have a large and lucrative business. If, on the other hand, PCs continue to dominate the market for small business computers, and workstations are more restricted to the engineering market, then Microsoft will continue to grow at a rapid rate. Consequently, Microsoft should always be under consideration as a growth stock.

Lotus, like Microsoft, capitalized early on the trend toward IBM-type PCs. Lotus 1-2-3, which is the most widely used and easily recognized spreadsheet package, is designed to work with Microsoft's operating system. It is a paradox therefore that Microsoft's own spreadsheet, Excel, is a direct competitor to Lotus. The newer versions of Lotus are very powerful and involve large "three-dimensional" spreadsheets with very sophisticated capability as far as macro instructions and other features are concerned. Excel from Microsoft, however, is just as capable. There is some question as to whether Lotus will continue to grow at a rate comparable to the growth of the industry. Lotus also has made its software available for the workstation universe and functions well on Sun workstations. Therefore, if workstations come to dominate the business small-computer market, Lotus will already be there with a capable offering. Nevertheless, some growth from Lotus can be expected in the future and it is always a stock worth considering. On the other hand, it is receiving stiff competition from Excel and Borland's Quattro Pro.

Borland International has grown very rapidly in the personal computer software field. This company had sales in 1985 of only approximately $12 million but sales have now grown to $113 million. At the same time, net income has increased from less than $1 million to nearly $12 million in the year ending March 1990. This company designs and markets computer software that also functions primarily under the MS-DOS operating system. The three principal products are "Paradox," a relational data base management system, and "Quattro Pro," made available in late 1989, which is an advanced electronic spreadsheet. Additionally, the company markets computer-language compilers such as "Turbo Pascal." Borland's new product, which is an advanced spreadsheet, has had terrific acceptance due to low price strategy (it is significantly cheaper than Lotus 1-2-3) and is causing the company to grow quite rapidly. Additionally, Borland has a new product it is developing in conjunction with Windows 3.0.

Borland is an interesting company in that it has developed very powerful products for the Microsoft operating system environment. Consequently, the company is growing extremely fast and the stock has been an excellent performer as well. It should be noted, however, that Borland has some litigation with Lotus concerning their products. This litigation may provide a barrier to the company's future growth if it is resolved unsuccessfully. Nevertheless, Borland is a company well worth looking at. A recently proposed merger with Ashton-Tate, a database softwear designer, will only make Borland stronger.

In addition to the software areas in companies I have mentioned there are a number of new technologies being developed that may play an important part in the growth of the software industry in the 90s. One of the most interesting, albeit slightly bizarre, is a concept known as "virtual reality" (VR). A great deal has been written on the subject of VR, although it is only in its infancy technologically. The concept is that by using very fast computers and very sophisticated software it is possible to simulate full interactive environments for people to enjoy, either for education, training, or recreation. This is done by encasing the user in a suit containing tiny liquid crystal displays in front of each eye for visual display, as well as sensors attached to computers by fiber optics to detect body movement. The illusion that is created is that the person is walking through an alien artificial environment called "cyberspace." As the person moves a part of his body, the sensors react and change the environment so that the person has the illusion that he is able to control the objects having "real" texture and weight in the visual environment. For example, sensors in the hand permit the person to reach out and have the illusion of grabbing objects that appear three dimensionally. Even sound will be supplied. This enables individuals to have the sense of walking through strange or unusual worlds. It combines sophisticated computer simulation with the potential for delivering training exercises, educational material, or hallucinatory experiences. For example, a medical student will be able to go "on a walk" through the human body. Obviously this technology will have many uses, some serious and some purely recreational. Nevertheless, as this technology emerges, it will generate significant revenues and profit for those companies able to exploit it. While there are no companies presently selling affordable VR systems, the systems do exist on an experimental basis and cost upward of $250,000.

As computers become more powerful and software more sophisticated, one can imagine this technology being affordable to business people. It is one of the more promising concepts for the later part of the decade, so investors should watch for companies involved with it. However, caution should be exercised because infant technologies frequently exist as stock fads long before commercialization. The leading companies at the fad stage frequently are eclipsed by other companies later on. The initial leader in digital watches (Pulsar) and hand-held calculators (Bowmar) are no longer dominant (or even evident) in their markets today.

In summary, the market for software as a way to make the very fast computers of the 90s more accessible and more desirable to business will be very rapidly growing. Currently, approximately 25 million personal computers, slightly more than half, serve American business. It is also estimated that 60 percent of all white-collar workers will have PCs in their offices by the end of 1991, compared to 7 percent in 1983. Business-oriented PCs, however, are not simply confined to the office. The majority of people with PCs at home use them for work rather than recreation. Also, to a much greater extent, PCs are being linked to one another. Some estimate that between 35 percent and 45 percent of all PCs are linked into networks today. Five years ago that percentage was extremely small.

Nevertheless, despite the vast proliferation of this kind of computer, the PC, like the human brain, is only being utilized to a very small percentage of its capability in the white-collar environment. Unlike the human brain, however, the PC is becoming increasingly more capable. As a consequence, there is a tremendous need to find a way to make use of this extraordinary resource.

This industry resembles cable television, which in the early 1980s had penetrated a large number of homes before there was any real programming for it. Once the medium was entrenched, however, it was followed quickly by a vast array of new kinds of programming (HBO, home shopping, MTV, CNN).

Thus, the fact that small computers are so ubiquitous in American life is pushing software designers into high gear to utilize their power. As a consequence, software development will be one of the fastest growing industries in the country over the rest of the decade, spawning a wide variety of excellent investment opportunities, some of which are small and unknown to the investing public at this point. Many companies are privately held at present and will be brought public over the next five years. Special attention should be given to any software companies as they become public because this will be an extremely vital investing area.

An excellent example of how more powerful personal computers can combine with specifically targeted software to fill a business need and create a new fast growing company is found in CIS Technologies, Inc. While CIS Technologies (CIS) might more properly be found in the chapter under medical technologies, I put it in this chapter because investors should take note of this kind of company emerging during the 90s. This company illustrates how the power of the PC is being used by people who are familiar with a specific industry's needs.

CIS is actually only four years old. It was created by two accountants with computer expertise who were asked to help Aetna process Medicare claims. When hospitals file Medicare claims with the government they are not actually administered by the government but by fiscal intermediaries who are paid by the government to administer the claims. Typically these intermediaries are large insurance companies, but it varies from region to region. One of the problems facing hospitals is that getting the government to pay claims against the Medicare system has become very complex. The forms have to be filed perfectly; otherwise they are rejected. Even under the best of conditions a claim could take in excess of 90 days to process. As a consequence, hospital receivables are very stretched out and the requirements for processing the claims are getting more complex and bureaucratic.

CIS attaches a powerful PC to the hospital's mainframe. This PC receives electronically all of the billing information from the mainframe and checks the information for accuracy and consistency so that it will pass through the Medicare bureaucracy without any problem. It creates a suspense file of bills that are incorrectly labeled or have other problems. These problems can vary widely; in some cases it is a miscoding; in other cases, a doctor's signature is lacking, etc. The bills are then forwarded electronically to CIS' data processing facility in Tulsa, Oklahoma, and there reformatted into the form required by the payor (whether it is the Medicare fiscal intermediary or a third party payor such as an insurance company). Insurance companies require that bills submitted be in their particular format; CIS' computers in Tulsa have templates for the preferred format for most insurance companies in the country.

This process has the effect of substantially reducing average hospital receivables; in some cases by as much as 30 days. At the same time, it has allowed hospitals to reduce their clerical staff associated with getting the government and other payors to process claims. At present, the company is still small, with revenues for this year estimated to be approximately $20 million. Nevertheless it is growing extremely rapidly and we expect that it will continue to grow at a rapid rate for the next several years, although it is constrained by the availability of qualified personnel. While it is itself an investment worth considering by growth stock investors, CIS is more important as a paradigm; it has created a business that did not exist five years ago; this was made possible by the PC and specifically targeted software.

Growth stock investors should look for this kind of investment as there will be a proliferation of smaller software companies capitalizing on what are known as vertical (one product area) markets and growing very rapidly. The *New York Times* (February 10, 1991) reports that even choreographers such as Merce Cunningham are using computers for creating and recording dances. While this will not be interesting from a business viewpoint, it shows how greatly our lives will be altered by newly developed computing capabilities. Thus, software development is going to be one of the fastest growing industries in the United States over the 90s and many companies have the capability to capitalize on these rapidly evolving trends. CIS is but one example.

KEY INVESTMENT POINTS

1. A software company can grow faster than almost any kind of company because it requires little investment in plant and equipment. Consequently, software companies are not burdened by the

need for capital or the time it takes to build factories. This enables them to have very high margins and be somewhat protected from the competitive pressures hardware companies experience. As a result, they can be great stocks, growing very rapidly from a small size.

2. Software will be the regulator of the data processing industry growth in the 90s. As a result, many stocks will benefit.

3. Writing software is difficult and time-consuming; products are highly proprietary and hard to copy. Also the United States has a distinct edge in software versus the rest of the world. The Japanese are behind in software development because of the complexity of their own written language. Therefore these companies are less volatile than many hardware producers. As a result, the companies frequently deserve and get high multiples. They are frequently good investments, nevertheless.

4. There will be many software growth stocks during the 90s that will be excellent investments. Because of their characteristics they can emerge as if from nowhere. Find a broker whose analysts know this industry; it will be a great place to concentrate.

CHAPTER 15

HOW TO INVEST IN DATA PROCESSING STOCKS

As a rule, data processing stocks, are exceptionally volatile. Consequently, there is always the opportunity to make a substantial profit in specific stocks in this group. However, there are a number of rules to be followed by investors in these stocks. Following are a list of dos and don'ts.

DON'Ts

1. Don't allow yourself to become overly impressed, mesmerized, or confused by technology; remember that technology is simply a means to an end. A computer can be the fastest in the world, but if there is no software for it, there will be no market for it either. A semiconductor can be the most advanced, but if the computer manufacturers refuse to adopt it because they are standardized on some other format, it will be commercially unsuccessful.

I am familiar with a company that claims to be able to produce a computer on a single sheet of material that looks essentially like Saran wrap. There is a fair amount of evidence that this indeed can be accomplished. On the face of it, this seems like an amazing accomplishment: If you need a computer, simply take out your sheet of plastic, roll it out on the desk, and go to work! What this ignores is that such a computer is extremely hard to produce, and it does not fit in with other forms of computers. As a result, it has limited commercial value.

Most data processing solutions are evolutionary rather than revolutionary. They take a known technology and extend it just a little bit further, making it slightly smaller, faster, and more capable. Moreover, hardware solutions always have to pause and wait for software solutions to catch up to them. While it is true that the most exciting growth stocks are companies that have not been around for many years, it is important to note that typically their products fit into the generally accepted framework. For example, the Sun workstations took a concept, RISC architecture, and an operating system UNIX, both of which were already well known, and combined them to make a product (workstations) to fit into a market already pioneered by several other companies. Thus, while the company was new, and it refined several well-known ideas, none of the technologies was revolutionary.

Another example is the Apple Macintosh. The GUIs (graphical user interface) which were such a powerful sales feature for the Apple Macintosh had actually been pioneered several years before by Xerox. Thus, the technology was not revolutionary, simply the application and marketing of it. Xerox, the inventor, was not the company that capitalized on the development. This frequently happens.

2. Avoid stocks that are pioneers in a brand new technology, until they have sales and earnings. In Chapter 14, we mentioned that the pioneers of new technologies frequently are not the companies bringing them to full development and to ultimately dominate the market. There are many examples of this; some new technologies develop into stock market fads with lots of little companies seizing on the idea well before the concept is commercially viable; artificial intelligence is an example. It is my guess that "virtual reality" will be a concept like this.

It takes a long time to bring a new area of technology to full commercial fruition. For example, the fax machine was available for years prior to the mid-80s. However, it was not until the mid-80s that the product developed a sufficient critical mass so that it became ubiquitous in the American office. There are numerous reasons for this. The first is that early versions of a product usually don't work very well. Not only do they not do what they are supposed to do, but they also have a tendency to break. When they break, there is frequently an absence of dealer support to fix the product. Thus, new products are quickly adopted by the few people who love gadgets, but not generally by the larger consumer or business markets. It is only when the concept is nearly perfected in the marketplace that the real expansion takes place. Consequently, the companies that often benefit are not the pioneers, but those able to commercialize, manufacture, and support the new product.

It has frequently been said of the Japanese that they are not inventors; but once a product is in the market they are capable of producing and marketing the product better and cheaper than their American counterparts.

There is a great deal of truth to this. The Japanese did not invent mass production for the automobile, the television set, or the D-RAM, but few could argue that they are capable of producing all the products cheaper and better than most other countries of the world. Never disregard the potential for Japanese competition in data processing hardware. This contrasts with the biotechnology or pharmaceutical industries, where enforceable patents are available to protect small pioneering companies from their competitors. Also, in most areas in the medical industry FDA approval must be obtained. Other laws, such as the Orphan Drug Act also serve to create barriers to entry and protect smaller companies. Thus, smaller pioneering companies can grow to full maturity in a regulatory cocoon. However, no such cocoon exists in the data processing industry. Software, however, is slightly more protected, partially because it is easier to keep its technology secret. Whereas machines can be dismantled and copied, software cannot. Also, because Western languages lend themselves more easily to software development, the competition from the Japanese is far less intense.

3. Data processing stocks generally move on their earnings, so buy stocks whose earnings are growing at a very rapid rate. However, if earnings growth slows, these stocks fall from favor very quickly. One of the anomalies of this group of stocks is that they tend to sell at very high multiples of peak earnings and low multiples of trough earnings. Notice that in bigger, more mature companies the opposite is true. This phenomenon occurs because data processing companies are accorded growth stock multiples after they have had a period of sustained earnings increases. Should there be an earnings shortfall, however, the company is stripped of its growth stock designation by the investment community. The multiple drop can be very substantial. Consequently, it is important to monitor quarterly earnings progress very closely and eliminate a stock at the first sign of trouble. Conversely, it is important to invest in companies that seem to have strongly accelerating earnings growth.

If the company is undergoing a product transition, as is frequently the case, the stock should be, generally speaking, sold until the product transition is complete. A product transition means that the company is replacing its old model with a new model. During this time customers generally hold off buying both the old model (because the new model is coming) and the new model itself (because it is not yet available). This causes substantial earnings declines on a quarterly basis and the stocks can drop substantially. On the other hand, sometimes it is a great time to buy a data processing stock *after* it has had the product-transition stock decline because earnings will reaccelerate when the new product comes on stream. However, when a company is undergoing a product transition, the products are frequently delayed. This should be monitored extremely closely. A smooth product transition is comparatively rare in this industry.

4. Data processing stocks tend to move together, so be careful when the industry is in the doldrums. When they are all doing well, even the weak companies can go up quite significantly. When they are all doing badly, even the best stocks will sometimes resist going up, even in the face of very strong earnings gains. An investor in this group should be very conscious of what the group as a whole is doing. If the group is in the doldrums, this is an excellent time to do research and buy stocks in anticipation of the next move. Sometimes it can take a while, however, before the next move in the group occurs. Nevertheless, when it occurs, it usually happens like an explosion rather than a series of sequential events. At this point it will be too late to begin to do research into the group because the stocks will be moving upward at a very rapid rate; picking between stocks will be more difficult because there is very little time. After the group has moved significantly, the market will begin to differentiate between the good and the bad ones. It is important to make sure that your portfolio only consists of companies that are fundamentally sound, because after the first kneejerk group move, companies with less than sound fundamentals tend to give up their profits quickly.

DOs

1. Do look for companies that are growing rapidly and have sound commercial products. It is more important to know how a company's products fit into the market they are serving than how they actually work. It is always useful to talk to users of the product to find out why they like them. Discussions with salespeople at computer stores (such as Computerland) are also a good way to get the product information. Remember that a businessman looks at data processing as a tool; the tool has to be effective not only in accomplishing its job, but it must also be reliable, have available maintenance, have flexibility (which may mean a lot of software), and fit in with the other products that the company owns.

2. Look at the company as a whole. The better companies generally will win. This means the companies with the best marketing management and financial health—not necessarily the most advanced products. In the war between Digital Equipment and Data General, two rivals in the minicomputer business (which was a growth industry in the 1970s and early 1980s), Digital Equipment often beat out Data General even though Data General's computers were frequently faster. This was because Digital Equipment had the better, stronger organization in areas such as software, maintenance support, marketing, and finance.

3. In general, it is better to focus on the simple rather than the complicated. Investors like simple stories. The more complex the story, the more it will turn off other investors and make the stock less desirable. One of the best stocks of 1969 was Milgo Electronics, a company that produced modems. Modems are devices that allow computers to communicate with one another over phone lines. In the late 60s, modems were just beginning to be universally used. Milgo was a hot stock because investors, both sophisticated and unsophisticated, could grasp in one sentence the appeal of the story. "A modem is a box which allows a computer to talk to another computer." Most people understood intuitively that this was going to be a very large market. Of course it is not recommended that an investor should invest on one-liners. The market has become far too sophisticated for this kind of approach. However, the stocks of simple good companies are frequently the best stocks to buy.

4. An excellent way to invest in data processing stocks is through mutual funds that specialize in them. These sector funds are available and are probably more capable of keeping up with the rapidly changing technologies than is an individual investor. Also, they provide diversified portfolios, which is especially important in this group. One should always maintain a diversified portfolio of technology stocks because if there is a slight shortfall in the earnings of the stock it is not uncommon for the stock to plunge in excess of 30 percent in a couple of days. To avoid one stock taking down an entire portfolio, diversification is extremely important.

Despite the advantages of sector funds, the stocks in this group tend to move together. Consequently, sector funds can have short periods of fantastic performance followed by periods of significant underperformance versus the popular averages. Therefore another approach is to buy good growth funds whose job it is to pick among the various growth sectors. Good growth funds will move into data processing stocks when the time is right and, after they have been exploited, move into other growth areas, such as the medical stocks.

In summary, data processing stocks are seductive, scary, and can be very profitable. Over a number of years, an investor in these companies will probably come away accepting the veracity of the old Wall Street expression "no pain, no gain," or the equally valid, "no guts, no air medals."

In the chapters on data processing, I have included the names of numerous stocks. It is important to recognize that these are *not* recommendations. By the time this book is published a number of months will have passed since I wrote these chapters. Consequently, the stocks may have significantly different valuations. Moves in data processing stocks frequently take place in a matter of several months and, consequently, perhaps none of these companies will be interesting investments by the time the book is published. Also, the fundamentals of the companies may have changed. These companies, however, provide a good place to begin looking. An investor should do his own research into these companies and then apply the standard of valuation provided in the book, or any other standard of valuation he chooses. As always with data processing stocks, caveat emptor!

CHAPTER 16

COMMUNICATION IN THE 90s

The way we communicate with each other, both personally and in business, will change substantially during the decade. Some of the newer technologies that will be fully developed have already appeared on the scene. Others will follow in an evolutionary way. Among the technologies we see as most prominent in the 90s are *voice mail*; its cousin, *interactive voice response*; and *cellular communications*. These technologies will not be stand-alone as they are now. By the end of the decade it is expected they will all be incorporated into other systems. Moreover, as we have discussed in Chapter 15, computers themselves will play a large part in this emerging communications network.

At present, however, each of these elements is discrete and the companies that provide them are not yet joined together in a corporate, marketing, or technological sense as they may be in the future. Therefore, it is important to look at these elements individually. As integration of these different formats evolves, newer technologies will be emerging to facilitate it.

VOICE MAIL

One of the technologies that is spreading the fastest is *voice mail*. Voice mail is just starting to become noticeable in all aspects of our society. One company has surged to the most prominent independent position in voice mail: Octel Communications. Octel had less than $1 million in revenue in 1984 and less than $10 million in its fiscal year ending June 1986. However, in the year ending June 1990 the company had $127 million in revenue. In 1986 the company made less than half a million dollars net income, in 1990 it made almost $18 million. This parallels and defines the emergence of the industry.

Octel produces voice mail systems (also known as voice processing). A system of this kind allows a corporation to add a module to its phone system to serve as an answering machine for every party on the system. A caller can therefore leave a message on the phone answering system that can be retrieved at a later point. Similarly, a person within the office can leave interoffice memoranda in any electronic "mailbox."

This technology does not sound very sophisticated; indeed, it sounds very much like a conventional phone answering system of the kind most people have in their houses. There is a difference, however. A normal phone answering system works on an analog basis; it simply records the information on a tape and replays it. The Octel system digitizes the address and handles it in digital form. As a consequence, the Octel system is far more flexible. It can, for example, send the same message to all of the parties on the system or even externally at a predetermined interval. Digitizing enables a system to handle and route simultaneously a large number of messages. It allows executives to create and store a list of other executives to whom messages can be sent.

The advantage of such a system is that it confers the ability to have a "one-sided" phone conversation. When all businesses have these systems, the need for a secretary or receptionist taking messages will be completely eliminated. This will reduce errors; but, more importantly, "the ping-pong" phone call will also be eliminated. An individual can leave a message in a person's voice mail box and the person can respond to it by leaving a return message in the caller's mailbox. No actual two-way conversation ever need take place. This makes salesmen more productive, for example; no leads are lost, no potential customers need remain uncontacted. Also, the fact that these messages are digitized allows a large number of them to be stored, sequenced, and replayed in any imaginable sequence. A person could replay his incoming messages in terms of time, or theoretically, by key words.

While the Octel-like system does not seem revolutionary, it is surprising how infrequently it is now found in a business context and yet how greatly it improves productivity.

Within five years voice mail systems will probably be as ubiquitous as fax machines are today. It is the potential for integrating voice mail with other forms of data processing hardware that makes it truly exciting. We have discussed the possibility that by the year 2000 computers will respond to voice commands and reply with voice synthesis. As the address on a voice mail system of the Octel type is digitized it is easy to imagine a personal computer that can act as the repository of voice information and also have the ability to make delayed phone calls.

It will probably be a feature of business, in the late 1990s, that a person will be able to dictate a message to his computer. This message can be forwarded at a predetermined time to a business associate. It may include data taken from the computer and converted to voice. For example, a person might want to tell a colleague that there has been a change in a meeting schedule and include some new data about the meeting. However, the first person only receives this information at 11:00 PM. Not wanting to disturb his colleague until the beginning of business hours (9:00 AM the next morning) he dictates the phone message to his computer, the computer "wakes up" at 9:00 AM the next morning, relays the message verbally to the colleague. The colleague either receives the message in the form of a synthetic phone call or the message is stored in the colleague's voice mail box. This would be, essentially, a one-sided voice memo. Using this tool, an executive could also communicate to a large number of staff members at the same time. Without knowing which parties were available, a conference call could be held with the initiator absent.

Another feature of modern communications is the development of *voice response systems* (VRS). VRS works as follows: It channels a phone call down a menu of possibilities, eliminating the need for costly human interface. Doubtless, you have experienced a VRS. It sounds something like this: "This is First Central Bank, if you want your balance, press 1; if you want to find out the latest interest rates on our CDs, press 2; if you want to talk to a human being, press 3."

Multiple branching with VRS is possible. Indeed, if the repondent were to press 1, he might get another menu saying, "If your balance is in checking, press 1; if in savings, press 2." If he presses 1 again, he might be asked to go down another branch. This kind of system has become very popular with large institutions. VRS is a technology not unlike voice mail. Indeed, some of the voice mail companies, such as Octel, are moving to enter the VRS market. Obviously, there is substantial potential overlap between the two. Also, VRS can be combined with voice mail.

Two companies have led the way in the development of VRS: Intervoice, Inc., and Syntellect, Inc. Both of these companies generate revenues in the range of $20 million, which is excellent growth when one considers that this industry did not exist at all in 1985. While profits of these companies may be affected by the present recession, it is nevertheless true that this kind of company should be regarded as interesting as a part of the fabric of the communications system of the 90s.

CELLULAR COMMUNICATIONS

The communications industry that has the greatest potential for growth in the 90s is cellular communications. Most people are familiar with cellular telephones, despite the fact that at the end of 1990, there were only about 5 million subscribers. Nevertheless, if one were to compare the development of cellular telephone systems to a child's education, the industry would now be in about fifth grade.

The industry began its commercial existence in 1985. In the early 80s the FCC (Federal Communications Commission) gave out cellular franchises for all of the major markets in this country. All major markets have two franchises. The first is the "wireline" system, which is owned by a local phone operating company (usually a Regional Bell Operating Company, such as NYNEX); the second is an independent franchise. It was believed that by having two franchises, the competition between them would be sufficient to keep pricing reasonable as the industry grew.

By the end of 1985 there were 340,000 subscribers. Since then, the rate of growth in subscribers has been consistently very high. By the end of 1990, 84 percent of the population had available cellular service despite the low penetration. Recently, cellular licenses were awarded for rural service areas (RSAs). Recipients are required to build out their systems by the end of 1992. As a result, we expect that at the end of 1992, approximately the entire country, 245 million people, will have cellular service available.

A cellular system involves complex technology. Mobile phones communicate with cells that receive the call and connect it to the phone system. As the subscriber moves from cell to cell, a computer hands the call off to the next cell. When working properly, this is seamless; a subscriber does not know when his call is being handed off. If the market is very dense, more cells are required. In a properly functioning system, even when calls are originating from automobiles traveling over 65 miles an hour, the system has no problem handing off the subscriber to the next cell.

Most of the growth of cellular telephones has been in the automotive market. (The little curlicue antennae frequently seen on cars on the highway are for cellular phones.) The first phase of the industry's development was oriented toward people driving. In 1985 a cellular system installed in a car cost about $1,000. Now car phones are available for under $200 and, increasingly, subscribers are switching to portable phones. Phones have been reduced in size and weight to the point where they can be carried comfortably in a briefcase or even in a pocket. Even the price of fully portable phones is coming down. The top-of-the-line portable now costs about $800, compared to $2,000–$3,000 only a few years ago. Because of the drop in the price of hardware, cellular phoning is becoming much more popular.

This technology however, is not simply limited to the United States. All over the world cellular phones are becoming a normal way of communicating. In some countries, the cellular phone industry has blossomed because the conventional phone industry is not as good as it might be. The Scandinavian countries have comparatively high penetration rates although not necessarily for the reason just given.

Initially it was thought that the only buyers for cellular telephones would be people who spend a great deal of their time in cars and require the ability to have mobile communication. Traveling salesmen were typically cited as an example, professions that had to have emergency calling capability, such as doctors, were another. Now, to a greater extent, the average person is getting a cellular phone. This is especially true in cities such as Los Angeles where people spend a great deal of time in their cars. However, since having instant access to communication is highly desirable, it is expected that as phones continue to come down in price they will attract a larger segment of the market.

Most estimates made by industry analysts maintain that the industry will grow to between 40 and 60 million subscribers by the year 2000. The lower of these estimates has the growth of subscribers, which has been above 60 percent for the last several years, slowing to the 40 percent range in 1991, into the high-to-mid 20 percent range by 1995, and into the teens for the rest of the decade. The more rapid projections maintain a consistent rate in the low twenties through the rest of the decade. The more aggressive number envisions a 22 percent penetration of the United States by the year 2000, the lower end projects a 14 percent penetration.

The faster growth rates anticipate more elasticity as the price of the service comes down in the last years of the decade. One way to estimate it is: There are approximately 110 to 120 million personal vehicles on the road. Car sales, including imports and light trucks, average around 10 million a year. Thus the fleet of cars turns over once every 10–12 years. I believe this fleet is conceptually divided into two kinds of car buyers: those who buy new cars and those who buy used cars. If one assumes that the average new-car buyer holds his car from four to five years, this would be consistent with the idea that the new-car buyer would then sell his car to the used-car buyer, who holds it another five to six years until it is scrapped. Therefore, 1991 model year cars will be held by their original owners until 1996 on average and will be on the road through the end of the decade. Many automobile companies are now prewiring cars for cellular phones in the expectation that their customers will buy phones along with their cars as a standard accessory, like radios. If we assume that about half of all cars (and some light trucks) built from 1991 on will be equipped with cellular phones, less than 5 million will receive it in 1991, but 12 million should have it by 1992, (the original five plus three 1991 cars plus at least four from 1992), 15 million in 1993, 20 million in 1994, 25 million in 1995, and 50 million by the year 2000 (portables may substitute for wired-in phones).

In addition, *if* there are 10 million people with portable phones by 2000, then 60 million phones will certainly not be out of the question at that time. This simplistic model assumes that half of the affluent segment (new-car buyers) will want it but none of the less affluent (used-car buyers) will. Obviously, these are gross generalizations.

There are many factors, which could accelerate the demand for cellular phones. The first is improved battery technology. Many companies are working on longer-life, rechargeable batteries. Currently, the length of a possible phone conversation (approximately 70 minutes in the most expensive Motorola portable) is a limiting factor and diminishes the usefulness of portable phones. Eliminating the crowding of cells in urban environments is another factor. In New York City, for example, at certain times, in mid-town, it is difficult to get and/or stay connected to a cell.

Digital System Cellular Phones

One of the most important trends for cellular phones will be the shift from analog to digital systems that will occur by 1995. Presently there are several competing digital technologies, but once the industry has standardized, the shift to digital could occur rapidly. The first possibility is a simple enhancement of the analog system that adapts some of the digital technology. Second, there is a time division multiple access (TDMA), and third, code division multiple access (CDMA). TDMA increases the amount of available cells by 5 to 10 times. CDMA increases by a higher factor.

Digital should have a stimulative effect on the market. It will enable the providers to expand their capacity greatly and give better service, clearer connections, better handoffs between cells. More importantly, it will enable cellular phones to interact with computers in an improved way. This permits the possibility of cellular phones as an extension of office voice mail systems. It also permits cellular phones to be attached to fully portable fax machines. Lastly, during the latter half of the decade, I believe that cellular phones will be extremely important input devices for computers.

As computers will be able to receive both input commands and data from the human voice by the end of the decade, the ability of a cellular phone to transmit this information to a computer in digital form will essentially free an individual from the computer itself. The phone will be able to be hooked up to a printer or small flat panel terminal without the need for a keyboard and will be able to receive input. One can imagine an executive in a limo dictating a letter by cellular to a computer, editing it, and then sending it by voice mail, electronic mail, or fax, without any human interface.

Near term, the tie-in between voice mail and cellular phones will be an important tool for business. The great productivity enhancement that voice mail offers by permitting the one-sided phone conversation, becomes even more effective if one is able to access voice mail from a remote location.

Cellular Phone Companies

Companies which operate cellular telephone systems have somewhat homogenous economic characteristics. Typically, customers generate about $82 a month in phone bills. This has come down slightly as newer subscribers tend not to use the systems as much as the hard-core businessmen who have had systems for some time. Nevertheless, there is a predictable similarity of revenues from system to system, depending on penetration.

Also cellular phone operators do have other industry-specific homogenous characteristics. For example, it costs a great deal of money, initially, to build a system and these costs must be borne at first by an extremely small customer base. Once the system is up and running, however, each subscriber usually provides a substantial amount of incremental operating profit. Operating expenses are no more than about 20 percent to 25 percent of revenues in a typical cellular system. General administration expenses can run to about 20 percent of the system as well, and marketing expenses can also be 20 percent to 25 percent of revenue because of the high commissions paid to salesmen to attract customers. Nevertheless, prior to interest and depreciation, margins can frequently be in the 60 percent range for a more mature system as marketing expenses slow.

The major single expenses in a system however, are depreciation, which is substantial because of the large capital cost associated with building the system, and interest expense for the same reason. Because of these two items, most cellular systems are, at present, unprofitable on the pretax profit line but not necessarily unprofitable from a cash flow standpoint (because depreciation is such a big expense item).

With these kinds of financial characteristics, the astute analyst will notice immediately that the leverage in a company of this sort is very great; cellular telephone systems have such a high percent of fixed costs that, once they pass break-even, profits will increase at an extremely rapid rate, much faster then revenues.

If by the year 2000 there are 60 million subscribers in this country, then over 20 percent of the industry's potential market will be paying customers. Given that each market has two systems, this suggests a market penetration for the average cellular company of more than 10 percent of the market. One analyst has estimated that at an 8 percent penetration rate the average cellular company will earn 40 percent net after tax on revenues. This estimate incorporates a fairly significant drop in average monthly revenues per subscriber and a full tax rate. Obviously, under such a scenario, the growth of net income past break-even would be extremely rapid. Consequently, it is possible that the cellular telephone industry will become one of the fastest growing industries in terms of earnings per share during the decade of the 90s.

Cellular Phone Stocks

Cellular telephone stocks have already had very significant upside moves over the last five years, although 1990 was not a good year. Nevertheless the stocks have done well, considering that few of the companies actually earn any money.

Typically, cellular telephone stocks trade on a basis of dollar per POP. POP stands for population (in the company's service area) and there are certain values attributable to a certain population size. Obviously some markets are more desirable than others and this will be reflected in the per

POP value. However, values are fairly homogenous and depend in part on the prices at which private systems trade. During the next few years, some of the cellular telephone companies will begin to achieve profitability. Once this has occurred, valuations can be put on earnings rather than on POPs. Initially, of course, P/Es will be extremely high because earnings will be very small. However, the leverage in cellular telephone companies is so great that the earnings growth could be spectacular and hence deserving of very high multiples.

The following companies are publicly traded non-wireline companies, ranked in order of net POPs: McCaw Cellular, Lin Broadcasting, Metro Mobile, Cellular Communications, US Cellular, and Vanguard Cellular (see Table 16-1). Additionally, some smaller companies that are publicly traded have wireline POPs and represent potentially interesting investments. They are: Centel, Contel, and Telephone and Data. The large Bell Regional Operating Companies are also major participants in the cellular business. In order of POPs they are: Pactel Cellular, Bellsouth, Southwestern Bell, Bell Atlantic, NYNEX, and Ameritech.

Of all the companies, McCaw Cellular is by far the largest. McCaw has been built by very substantial borrowing; consequently it is a company that is extremely leveraged. If this strategy is successful, McCaw will be extraordinarily profitable in the latter part of the decade. However, because of very substantial interest payments, it probably will take longer to achieve profitability than will some of the others. Lin Broadcasting, which is partially owned by McCaw has a very high valuation per POP because of its ownership of the Metro One franchise in New York City as well as the non-wireline franchise for Los Angeles.

Some of the smaller companies are extremely interesting. Among them, Vanguard Cellular, Century Telephone, and Metro Mobile stand out.

It should be noted that valuations change among the different cellular companies. It is extremely important for the investor in this group to look at the values both on the per POP basis and on a potential earnings basis at the point in time that the investment is going to be made; relative valuations change and the relative successes of the companies change. It is also important for an investor to have a diversified portfolio of cellular telephone companies to spread the risk. One way to do this is to invest in a sector fund that specializes in either communications technology or in cellular directly. Again, a good diversified growth mutual fund probably will have some participation in cellular stocks.

TABLE 16–1
Cellular Phone Companies

Company	Symbol	MSA POPs[1]	RSA POPs[1]	Total POPs[1]	Value: Noncellular Assets[2]	Net Debt[2]	Shares[2]	Price 2/19/91	Market Value per MSA POP	Market Value per Total POPs
				Independent Cellular Companies						
McCaw Cellular	MCAWA	59.5	0.0	59.50	$560.84	$5,559.49	178.54	$23.50	$154.53	$154.53
Racal	RTG	54.2	4.8	58.95	170.0	0.0	100.0	60.75	109.05	100.17
Lin Broadcasting	LINB (51.9-MCAWA)	26.4	0.0	26.44	676.0	1,640.4	51.4	66.25	165.21	165.21
Contel Cellular	CCXLA (90%-CTC)	18.9	3.6	22.48	0.0	1,312.8	100.0	19.50	172.45	145.11
Metro Mobile CTS	MMZB	10.9	0.0	10.87	74.9	718.3	63.1	13.50	137.61	137.61
Cellular Comm.	COMM	7.3	2.6	9.89	0.0	68.5	39.6	32.25	184.46	135.97
U.S. Cellular	USM (86.1-TDS)	8.4	1.1	9.50	0.0	1.3	28.5	18.63	63.35	56.02
Vanguard	VCELA	5.2	0.0	5.20	0.0	130.0	20.7	23.38	117.88	117.88
				Independent Telcos						
Centel Corporation	CNT	14.4	1.3	15.70	3944.4	1478.4	84.0	33.88	26.26	24.09
Telephone Data	TDS	7.2	3.6	10.79	907.9	190.9	30.5	33.63	42.81	28.69
Century Telephone	CTL	3.5	1.3	4.82	864.3	209.5	31.3	30.13	82.57	59.94

MSA: Metropolitan Service Area.
RSA: Rural Service Area.

[1]Millions
[2]Dollars millions
Source: Fred Alger Management, February 19, 1991.

KEY INVESTMENT POINTS

1. Communication companies are divided into two groups. First, there are companies that produce hardware/software products that enhance networks. These are similar to data processing hardware providers. Included would be vendors of voice mail and interactive voice response systems. This group is growing rapidly, dependent on R&D and new product flow, subject to cyclical influences and technology shifts. They sell on multiples of their earnings, like data processing stocks.

   The second group comprises service providers, cellular telephone companies, CATV companies, and conventional phone companies. These are either monopoly or quasi monopoly businesses and are frequently valued either on multiples of cash flow, yield, or some other method.

2. Cellular telephone companies have the potential to grow very rapidly during the 90s. However, they require massive up front set-up costs and heavy start-up marketing expenses. Consequently, most are unprofitable for many years. However, their monopoly status permits investors to project results very far into the future. Therefore, as most are without earnings, they trade on a basis of dollars per POP (people in their area). Within five years most should have earnings and will commence trading on a P/E basis. Because of the leverage inherent in the high fixed-cost nature of the business, once earnings begin they will grow at an extremely high rate. This could make these stocks very exciting in the latter part of the decade.

3. The communications world is circumscribed by a maze of Federal Communication Commission (FCC) regulations. This is a very specialized arcane area but it can often influence stocks significantly. It is often too complex for many laymen to grasp as it requires a great deal of research. As a result, I suggest that an investor might want to invest in this group through a sector fund. This will provide diversification and permit the assets to be managed by someone who keeps track of these rules on a full-time basis.

CHAPTER 17

SPECIALIZED GROWTH AREAS

In the 90s, there will be a number of less obvious areas of the economy that will contain rapidly growing companies. In some cases, they include having interesting niche participants that are growing rapidly even though their markets are stagnant. It is important to review these areas for two reasons. First, an investor should be conscious that growth stocks can be found anywhere; he should be aware of niche participants who are able to grow by altering slightly an accepted formula. Secondly, investors should be aware that the social trends they read about in the newspapers can frequently be the spawning ground for interesting stock market investments. When there is a problem, especially a problem of sufficient magnitude that it is covered in the newspaper, there are entrepreneurs who want to make money by finding the solution.

ENVIRONMENTAL CLEANUP STOCKS

The first area, environmental cleanup, is about a problem very evident in the United States and also becoming a concern throughout the world. One would suspect that a problem of this magnitude would have lots of publicly traded companies trying to make money by solving it. However, there are regulatory obstacles to making money in this effort. Also, for all the publicity the problem gets, there is not much money allocated to improving the environment and, consequently, it has not been a vast spawning ground for great growth companies. Occasionally, a fad related to cleaning up the environment, such as asbestos abatement, will cause a number of small companies to have violent upside stock moves. However, few of these concepts have translated into revenues and profits to any great degree. As a result, as far as investments are concerned, these fads frequently die at birth or after modest growth. Nevertheless, some elements of this industry that will provide interesting investments during the 90s are described here.

One of the most notable features of the 90s, is that we are creating a very substantial amount of waste every year and this waste must be dealt with. Very generally, waste can be divided into two categories, solid waste (garbage) and toxic or hazardous waste. Both of these represent problems that will grow more acute during the decade. Consequently, both of them represent opportunities for companies to make a great deal of money.

Probably one of the most threatening problems with solid waste is that we are using up our landfills; by the year 2000, we will have exhausted approximately one-third of the nation's total capacity. If this occurs, communities will have to fight one another for disposal space and the cost of disposal will escalate. It is expected that the total tonnage of garbage will rise from approximately 158 million tons in 1988 to 193 million tons by the year 2000. Some studies estimate that 50 percent of this tonnage will either be recycled or converted into waste energy by the year 2000. This compares to approximately 25 percent in 1988. Nevertheless, despite the fact that landfill usage will decline from 75 percent of total volume in 1988 to 50 percent in the year 2000, the actual volume of usage will not be down that much, 97 million tons versus 120 million. Current construction rates are estimated to add only 4 million tons per year of new capacity. As a result, companies that are either building new disposal sites or in a position to control existing disposal sites will show very substantial growth in the future.

The most important company in the waste disposal industry has already been a major growth stock over the past 10 years. In 1980, Waste Management had revenues of $560 million. At year end 1989, the company had grown to $4.5 billion. Net income in the same period had accelerated from $55 million to $560 million, a tenfold increase. Waste Management collects, processes, and disposes of solid waste in 48 states. At the end of 1989 it served about 800,000 commercial and industrial companies and 8.1 million households. It also operated 126 landfills. Additionally, Waste Management owns 77 percent of Chemical Waste Management, which is the largest provider of hazardous waste disposal. Waste Management's business is basically collecting and disposing of garbage. However, it has been able to apply technology, capital, and know-how to doing this more efficiently than its competitors. While it seems like a prosaic activity, the company continues to grow at 15 percent per year. This breaks down as follows: 8 percent is from increased volume, 5 percent from increased prices, and the rest from acquisitions. Part of the increased volume comes from Waste Management's successfully negotiating contracts with new municipalities; it is able to do this because it has achieved such great economies of scale that it is able to underbid most companies adjacent to its service areas.

Most importantly, Waste Management is profiting because of the substantial margins associated with its landfills. In the old days, landfills were nothing more than huge pits or places in the water where garbage was dumped. Now landfills have to conform to the very exacting Environmental Protection Agency standards, as well as to local and state environmental laws. Frequently, the local and state laws are more strict than the federal laws. Moreover, these rules are being tightened. There are rules that require double lining of the pits, as well as the ability to vent methane gas, for example. Building a new landfill requires not only a large area of undeveloped land, but the ability to steer the landfill through the myriad of regulatory approvals. Substantial capital has to be invested in a site before it can be approved. Consequently, big companies such as Waste Management can continue to grow in this business because they can afford to invest the capital and have the know-how necessary to get landfills approved.

The following charts (Figures 17–1, 2, 3, and 4) supplied by the Environmental Protection Agency show the drop in disposal capacity. This drop is of sufficient magnitude that the pricing for the use of landfills will rise substantially by the year 2000. Notice that in two of the models, the required landfill capacity crosses over the available capacity prior to the year 2000; it is only with very substantial amount of recycling activity that the two meet at the year 2000. I've included as well, a map that shows the severe nature of the landfill crisis in the Eastern part of the United States. This suggests that companies deriving a significant portion of their profits from landfills, especially in the East, will have earnings that will accelerate rapidly toward the end of the decade. Waste Management is a good example.

Another company that should be a major beneficiary of the trend toward environmental concern is Chambers Development. Chambers Development has 10 landfills currently permitted but should have 16 by the end of 1992. This alone should ensure financial growth for the company at least through the mid-90s.

One of the issues not yet being addressed by this industry is nonhazardous industrial (nonresidential) waste. Nonhazardous industrial waste is estimated to be five to seven times the volume of municipal waste.

FIGURE 17–1
Most Landfills Will Close Their Gates

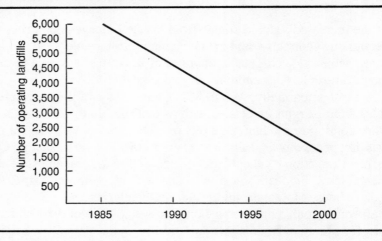

Source: EPA, *Report to Congress*, 1988.

FIGURE 17–2
Disposal Capacity Is Dropping

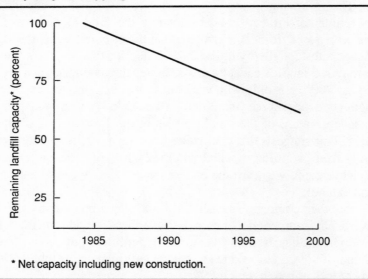

* Net capacity including new construction.

Source: EPA, *Municipal Landfill Survey*, 1986.

FIGURE 17–3
Landfill Capacity in the Year 2000

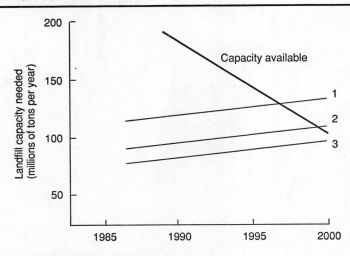

1. 15% of waste stream recycled
   15% of waste stream burned in resource recovery plants;
2. 25% recycled
   25% resource recovery;
3. 25% recycled
   35% resource recovery;

Source: EPA, *Municipal Solid Waste Landfill Survey*, 1986.

Presently, there are no regulations for disposal of this vast pile of waste materials; usually, it is simply stored at the industrial site where it is generated. One of the changes that may occur in the 90s is that industrial waste may have to go into double-lined landfills. This would be a bonanza for companies such as Waste Management and Chambers, both of which have substantial landfill capacity. Already Chambers is taking special industrial waste; municipal sludge that comes from sewers is an example. By December 31, 1991, New York City will no longer be permitted to dump sludge in the ocean. As a result of this kind of regulation there may be regional pockets where there is too much supply of specialized waste streams. Companies located in the East Coast, as is Chambers, may be ideal to solve this problem. We expect, of course, that it will be highly profitable.

FIGURE 17-4
State Landfill Capacity: The Changing Complexion of Waste Disposal

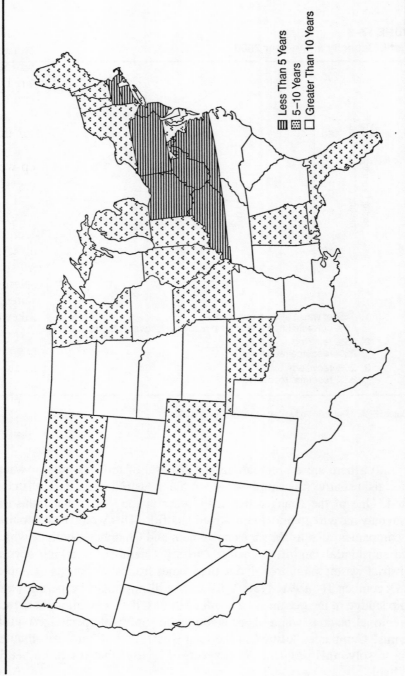

Less Than 5 Years
5–10 Years
Greater Than 10 Years

Source: National Solid Waste Management Association (NSWMA), 1988.

Another environmental concern is the treatment of hazardous waste. Most people are familiar with some of the hazardous waste horror stories, such as the infamous Love Canal in New York State. Since hazardous waste emerged as a major public concern during the 70s and 80s, there has been significant environmental legislation put into effect to regulate the flow of industrial toxic waste. At the same time a "Superfund" was created to clean out existing hazardous waste deposits. Despite all of this activity, not much has actually yet been accomplished.

There are four ways to handle a hazardous waste stream: deep-well injection, landfilling, incineration, and a new biotechnology approach. The first, deep-well injection, is the least desirable. This involves taking the hazardous waste and putting it down to the bottom of deep wells. While an easy solution, it is not a very popular one because it is uncertain whether the toxic waste will seep into the environment. Landfilling is another technique. However, landfills for toxic waste require a very substantial amount of capital, as the methods for controlling and regulating the flow of waste into the landfill are very stringent. The third, incineration, seems to be the most desirable as it can achieve what the EPA likes to call its "six nines," which means that .999999 of the toxic waste is eliminated in the burning process. Last, a new biotechnology approach is being attempted. Apparently there are microbes, some of which live on the floor of the Hudson river in New York, which actually like to eat PCBs.

Controlling toxic waste is not as easy or as profitable as one might think. Funding for toxic waste control has been more erratic in coming and the regulations surrounding it make it difficult and costly to do. Several companies, however, stand out in this effort.

Chemical Waste Management, which is a non-fully-owned-subsidiary of Waste Management, is probably the biggest operator in this industry; it uses all three methods of controlling the waste streams. Second largest is probably Rollins Environmental, which uses both landfills and incineration. Another company is Environmental Systems, which has a very large incineration complex in Eldorado, Arkansas, and has applied for one in Arizona.

These kinds of companies are frequently beset by regulatory problems. Very few people want a toxic waste incinerator near them or even in their own state, preferring to ship it to another state where the same problem exists. (Presently, Chemical Waste is having problems in Alabama.) This gives rise to some of the dirtiest municipal politics, and some of the companies in this industry have been touched by political scandals. Also, capacity tends to come on in big increments and the ability to increase earnings depends on obtaining approval for the next facility. However, the demand for this service exists and is growing constantly. Investors might do well to look at companies in this field. They should be aware, however that one can be hurt very badly by regulatory problems. Nevertheless, the enactment of the hazardous and solid waste amendments of 1984 to the Resource Recovery and Conservation Act (RRCA) will create a second round in growth of demand for this kind of company because it bans certain hazardous waste streams from normal landfill disposal.

During the course of the decade there will be other ways to participate in the environmental improvement industry. An investor should be very careful when examining companies in this business to make sure that they are able to implement their strategy without undue regulatory influence. Regulations in this industry can make profits extraordinarily lumpy and, as a consequence, some stocks sometimes are not the interesting investments that they first appear. Also, incinerating toxic waste or building a landfill is much more difficult to do well than it appears. Incinerators, for example, have to work within very fine tolerances in order to achieve maximum profitability; different types and grades of waste frequently alter the nature of the incineration process. Consequently, an investor should avoid any company that does not have a strong track record in this kind of activity. Also, this kind of company is very capital-intensive.

Companies with good organizations and lots of capital, such as Waste Management, will frequently end up dominating smaller, less well-managed companies. Therefore, while the environmental industry seems like it will have lots of potentially interesting investments, there aren't that many companies which actually exhibit strong growth for very long. However, the ones that do, such as Waste Management, can be superb investments. Indeed, Waste Management has been one of the countries' top growth stocks for the past 10 years. Presently trading around $36, the company's stock could have been bought at $1.50 in 1980.

The Soft Underbelly Play

The need to clean up the environment in the United States and elsewhere is mirrored by the need to clean up the human environment. Probably one of the fastest growth industries in the United States is crime. Surprisingly, however, there are very few public companies which address the problem of crime in America (and none that I know of that are involved in criminal enterprises, although the Mustang Ranch, a legal brothel in Nevada once did contemplate going public). Nevertheless, it is worth an investor's attention to watch for potentially emerging companies attempting to solve the problem of crime in the United States.

One of the few that have a solution to some aspect of this problem is BI Inc. BI is an interesting little company that is attempting to solve the overcrowding of the nation's jails and prisons. Court decisions have mandated that prisoners' rights and prison crowding be recognized. On the other hand, there is an accelerating growth rate in the number of prisoners (up 13 percent in 1989 alone) and little publicly available financing for new prisons. At present, the current capacity shortfalls will probably take three years to correct and taxpayers are understandably resistant to funding these projects.

BI is the leader in electronically monitored home-arrests systems (EMHA). The way EMHA functions is as follows: An offender on this system is typically a nonviolent prisoner, on parole or on work release; he works a full-time job and lives at home. His schedule is monitored by the corrections department or third-party monitoring company. This is accomplished by means of an ankle bracelet that contains a radio signal device. Should the subject leave his monitoring site the bracelet communicates with the host computer that he is gone; if he is not where he should be, efforts to track him down begin immediately.

EMHA was first introduced in 1984 and has been tested by many municipalities; currently about 20,000 people out of a pool of 7 million offenders are on EMHA. This number is growing rapidly as many states are converting from a trial basis to full usage and are expanding their system. Also, the federal government intends to expand its use of EMHA across the country.

BI has 65 percent of the market for unit sales and is also becoming a significant presence in third-party monitoring systems; we believe that BI will continue to dominate this market. Their equipment is superior to many of its competitors; it is tamperproof and an alarm is activated if it is removed in any way. There are numerous patents that protect its technology. Total revenues for BI are still small, approximately $18 million. However this is up from $1.5 million in the fiscal year ending June of 1987. We expect that the company will be able to grow during the next three to five years. This growth may be erratic, however, as BI depends on big contracts to grow. Quarterly earnings are frequently random and the stock is very volatile.

In addition to BI, there are several other companies in the (loosely defined) incarceration business. There are even several publicly owned chains of prisons. Nevertheless, the problem of crime is screaming for solutions, and I expect that during the next five years a number of companies may come public that exploit this very rapidly accelerating problem of crime in America. Many companies touch on it indirectly. Pinkerton, for example, is in the security business and has recently gotten a significant amount of attention because of the possibility of Iraqi-sponsored terrorism. Nevertheless, the private security business is not growing rapidly at present.

These kinds of companies relate to a problem with which most Americans are concerned about. Consequently, they can sometimes make excellent stock market investments. Investors should note that attempts to solve the crime problem are in a huge market, and a growing one, and will doubtless contain numerous lucrative investments during the decade, many of which are not even in the public market at present.

THE COOKIE CUTTER CONCEPT

One of the most interesting concepts in the stock market is the cookie cutter concept. Many fabulous investments have been derived from this idea, including McDonald's, Wal-Mart, and Toys R Us. The concept is simple: an entrepreneur develops a new format for selling a product (whether it is hamburgers, pizza, clothing, or appliances is irrelevant); the concept becomes successful; then the entrepreneur replicates the store concept at a rapid rate across the country.

There are so many companies that have at various times appeared to be on this kind of path, that an entire book could be written about just this kind of company. However, there are certain characteristics that all of these companies tend to have if they are going to be successful over a number of years. They are as follows:

Winners' Characteristics

1. Excellent site selection. Most companies that sell directly to the public have to have their units located in good, accessible areas. One of the factors that causes the fast-food industry to change is that neighborhoods change and yesterday's excellent site might be today's deteriorating neighborhood. Nevertheless, it is true that most companies that ultimately succeed have excellent site selection personnel. A recent example of this is Blockbuster Inc., which has been an extraordinary growth stock over the last five years. Blockbuster's site selection chief came from McDonald's, a company that is considered to be preeminent in site selection.

2. The concept must provide a better product or service than that which is being provided by existing units in the market. It is important that the company be able to differentiate itself from its competitors, because there are always a large number of emerging store chains. Two very good examples of this are Toys R Us and Blockbuster. Toys R Us is successful because it offered toys at a reasonable price but offered a much wider variety than was available in department stores. Department stores allocated a modest amount of space to toy sales; this square footage increased at Christmas time and shrank again during the rest of the year. Consequently, parents were not trained to go to department stores to find the best quality and widest selection of toys. However, at Toys R Us they knew they could find whatever toy was available on the market, at any time. As a consequence, they ignored the department store and went directly to Toys R Us. As the chain expanded it was able to dominate its competitors because of the size of the store and its selection. This drove department stores out of the toy business and put mom and pop stores into bankruptcy.

The second example is Blockbuster. Blockbuster had much the same idea as Toys R Us, it pioneered the video super store. Again, it provided much greater selection; whereas previous video stores only offered 3,000 to 5,000 titles, Blockbuster expanded to 10,000 titles. As a result, it was able to dominate the video rental store market. While these concepts seem fairly obvious in hindsight, it took a great deal of retailing savvy, capital, cost control, and site selection to make it actually happen on a large scale. Blockbuster opens a store a day nationwide and the organizational skill required to do this is not typically found in most American companies.

3. The third characteristic is cost control. No chain can grow rapidly without the ability to control every aspect of its costs at all times. All businesses require cost control, of course, but a rapidly expanding retail chain, which typically work on relatively small margins can quickly fly out of control if all aspects of the company's business are not tightly managed. As a consequence, financial management is of paramount importance in one of these concepts. A good management information system, a strong chief financial officer and a thorough knowledge of the business are extraordinarily important. Each type of business has its own cost accounting problems. Consequently, if one is investing in a relatively new chain it is important that the chain have solid management that comes from the specific industry, especially in the financial area. Without this, any chain concept will be doomed to failure and the ride in the stock market could be frighteningly brief.

4. The fourth requirement is pizazz. Pizazz is an intangible, but is easier to spot than one might think. It includes among other things a certain merchandising panache. The average person can detect this fairly easily by visiting the stores. It incorporates the whole concept, the advertising, the attractiveness of the units themselves, the cleanliness and appearance of the sales personnel, and their ability to deliver the product on time, in a nicely presented way. If the individual stores are sloppy or dirty, chances are the chain will not be a success. The chain should be able to reach out and grab its target market and really stand out in a merchandising sense. All of the great growth stocks of this kind have had marketing pizazz. McDonald's, Toys R Us, and Blockbuster are all examples.

5. The stores should have strong sales per square foot and strong sales per dollar of capital invested, per unit. These are two ratios that should be measured against other companies in the appropriate industry. They are easy numbers to obtain; the annual report or prospectus (in the case of a new offering) will provide the number of stores in the chain and the number of square feet per store. Usually, the dollar amount required to open a store is also available. This number is extremely important because ultimately the profitability of each individual store translates strongly into the profitability of the chain as a whole. It is important when making these calculations, however, to compare apples to apples. For example, take care not to compare a restaurant chain that serves breakfast, lunch, and dinner to a restaurant chain that does not serve breakfast, or a restaurant chain that serves liquor to a chain which does not.

It is always important to look at these types of companies as though one was going to open one of the units. An investor should always ask himself this question: Would I want to own a franchise in this chain. If I only owned one, would it be a profitable venture for me? If an investor can conclude both in terms of hard numbers and in terms of general feeling that owning one unit would be a great deal, then chances are the chain as a whole will be successful.

Pizza, Anyone?

Three relatively small, fast-growing companies of this type are Uno's Restaurant Corporation, Sbarro's Inc., and Spaghetti Warehouse, Inc. Two of the companies sell pizza but in totally different formats. Uno operates and franchises casual dining, full-service restaurants under the name Pizzeria Uno Restaurant and Bar. These restaurants serve gourmet, Chicago-style, deep-dish pizza, as well as numerous other entrees. Additionally, they serve liquor and are oriented toward a relatively affluent urban clientele in its 20s, 30s and early 40s (in other words, Yuppies). Uno has grown rapidly; in 1985, it had $10 million in sales, in 1990, we expect sales were $54.7 million. At year end 1985, it had 8 company-owned stores and 15 franchise stores. By the end of 1991, it should have 44 company-owned stores and 60 franchise stores. Uno's is located partially in the New England and the New York markets and, consequently, it is presently suffering slightly from the recession in those geographical areas. Nevertheless, it has been able to develop a very loyal clientele and will grow rapidly again in its market segment once the recession abates.

Sbarro's operates and franchises the largest national chain of Italian cafeteria-style restaurants. It offers pizza as well as other high-quality Italian specialties. Unlike Uno's, which is a more upscale restaurant, Sbarro is a small cafeteria-style, fast-food restaurant, usually located in shopping malls. Sbarro has demonstrated consistent growth and continuously strong comparable sales. Between 1982 and 1990, Sbarro expanded from 20 to 348 company-owned restaurants. In 1991 it expects to open another 60 or 65 restaurants. In terms of sales growth, sales were $5.5 million in 1982 and will approximate $22 million this year.

Another wonderful small company that fits the profile is Spaghetti Warehouse, Inc. This company operates 17 restaurants in 10 states. This chain has capitalized on the desire of the American family to eat inexpensively but in nice surroundings. As the name suggests, the company serves spaghetti and other classic Italian food and offers full alcoholic beverage service. The restaurants themselves are several times larger than a conventional restaurant (15,000 square feet) and can seat 450 people at a time. Prices are kept very low (about $8 for dinner per person). Nevertheless, sales per store, which average $2.8 million, are very high by restaurant standards because of the large seating capacity. The restaurants are also very profitable. The company has grown rapidly, from $15 million in revenues in 1986 to $43 million in 1991 (fiscal year ends in June), and we believe that Spaghetti Warehouse will be able to continue to grow rapidly during the 90s.

All three of these companies fit all of the requirements that we have outlined for successful companies. They have carved interesting and extremely profitable, fast-growing niches out of the restaurant market. In an industry that has the characteristics of being slow growing and oversaturated, these three companies continue to grow rapidly. An investor should keep in mind that despite the fact that there always will be a very large number of restaurant chains, new types of food served in different ways will always enable newer, fresher restaurant concepts to grow rapidly. These three should serve as models for the investor looking at similar formats.

Rising Retailers

The cookie-cutter concept is of course not confined to fast-food companies such as Uno's and Sbarro's. Some of the best stocks of this area have been retailers. Among them, Toys R Us, Wal-Mart, Gap Stores, and The Limited are companies that have grown very rapidly during the 80s and which have been extraordinarily profitable stocks. Wal-Mart has become an extremely large retailer, battling Sears for the title of largest retailer in America, the others also remain very fast-growing companies. Gap Stores continues to do extraordinarily well both in terms of its growth and in the stock market. Similarly, Toys R Us continues to be the dominant company in the toy market, and The Limited, though having a somewhat more erratic record than Gap Stores, continues to grow (in spurts) in the upscale apparel market.

Two companies, however, stand out as companies that could grow very rapidly in the 90s. The first is Home Depot. Home Depot will be a benefactor of the focus on home and family in the 90s. As we will discuss at greater length in Chapter 18, the 90s will be a period when the "baby-boom" generation matures into middle age. We believe that as a consequence home remodeling and do-it-yourself projects will be an increasingly important part of the housing industry. More importantly, Home Depot has found a format that seems to work extremely well. These stores specialize in building materials and home improvement as well as garden products. They are set up in warehouse format and range from approximately 60,000 square feet to in excess of 125,000 square feet. The new stores are typically 100,000 square feet or more. Additionally, these stores have outside selling areas, which can be from 10,000 to 15,000 square feet. The stores are basic in design but they are intended to create an image of efficiency and low prices. Merchandise ranges from lumber to hardware, electrical supplies, paints, and garden equipment. The company relies on very competitive pricing.

Home Depot has grown extremely rapidly in the 80s. In 1980 the company had only four stores; by 1990 the company was operating 145. Home Depot is geographically diversified and has stores in the Southeast, Northeast, Southwest, and also in California. The company continues to grow extremely rapidly; we expect sales in the 90s to grow at a rate in excess of 25 percent, with 20 percent or more coming from the addition of new square footage. Earnings also have grown at a rapid rate and we expect this to continue through the 90s. This company seems to be extremely well managed and increasingly is coming to dominate the do-it-yourself market in the areas in which it operates.

Another similar company is Office Depot, Inc. Office Depot and several other competitors took their concept from stores like Home Depot. Office Depot specializes in office products oriented toward smaller businesses which do not have the advantage of discounts from office product suppliers. This concept is relatively new; in 1986 the company only generated sales of $1.95 million, which compares with estimated sales in 1991 of $938 million. In 1986 the company had only three stores, but by the end of 1991, combined with Office Club stores, which it acquired this year, the company will have 182 stores. Presently, the chain is growing very rapidly with sales growing in excess of 45 percent. As the markets become more saturated, sales will probably slow down. However, we believe that the company can still grow at a rapid rate through the mid-90s. Office Depot has a strong presence in the Midwest, Southwest, and Southeast. The acquisition of Office Club gives it a dominant position on the West Coast.

Office Depot and Home Depot are two examples of rapidly growing retailers in market subsegments. Investors should be aware of companies of this kind but should only invest in their stocks after they have several years of track record so that management capability can be assessed. Frequently, two or three similar chains are started in different parts of the country and can grow very quickly until they come head to head in each other's markets. The better-managed chain usually will dominate. It is important, also, with retailers, that the company have very good control over its costs and its management information systems. Margins of retailers are traditionally very thin and if there are any accounting problems it will have a serious impact on the bottom line.

The most important research an investor in this kind of company can do, however, is to actually look at the stores themselves. Unlike biotechnology companies or data processing companies, this is where the investor's common sense can frequently be very helpful. If the store is attractive and offers good value it is an important positive; if not, don't buy the stock. Several large store chains, including Sears, have been penalized by not keeping up with the latest trends in pricing. Sears was very late to go to the "everyday low prices" concept, as was Zayre, which ultimately went out of business. It is extremely important, therefore, that stores be competitive in their prices. This is something that an investor can judge for himself at the store level.

Intuitive judgments should usually be followed in this group. Several years ago, Gap Stores changed its merchandising format from bright, colorful clothes to somber earth tones. It was obvious that the merchandise was much less attractive than it had been in the past. The company's sales fell off correspondingly and the stock plummeted. Upon realizing their mistake, the management corrected it and went back once again to its bright, appealing fashions. Sales came back rapidly and the stock did extremely well. No financial statements were needed to call these turns.

· On the other hand, investors cannot always understand or identify with the consumer products that are being sold in stores. A small chain, Merry-Go-Round, specializes in selling exotic fashions to teenagers. These fashions may be much more fashion-forward than the average investor might like to wear himself. Nevertheless, there is a market for them and Merry-Go-Round has grown quite rapidly over the last five years. Their products may not appeal to the investor, nevertheless, the investor has to recognize that there is a market for them and realize that the market may indeed be growing.

This example notwithstanding, cookie-cutter companies are generally selling their product to the public at large and common sense can play a great role in making sound investment judgments in this area. Investors should not underestimate the potential for making money from the cookie-cutter concept as a whole just because the companies are easier to understand than the more exotic areas such as biotech. Some of America's largest fortunes, including that of Sam Walton, the founder of Wal-Mart and richest American, have been made in this kind of business. The market usually rewards companies whose earnings growth is easily extrapolated into the future. This is the case with these companies, and consequently, they can generate considerable stockmarket excitement and profits.

KEY INVESTMENT POINTS

1. The cleanup of the environment will provide many interesting stocks during the decade. Landfill and toxic-waste disposal are two of the most obvious areas. While many of these companies can grow rapidly, they can sometimes have lumpy growth centered around the timing of regulatory approvals. In this group, the federal Environmental Protection Agency (EPA) and its rules do influence the industry, but frequently, state rules and politics can influence individual stocks more. Watch out for regulatory scandal, it has taken down more than one stock.

2. An investor should always talk to the state environmental regulatory authority where a company has a facility. Likewise he should always read the local papers. Local citizens frequently become hysterical when toxic-waste dumps or incinerators are being placed in their neighborhood. This can cause great disruption in corporate projects and, hence, earnings.

3. Despite these drawbacks, the stocks are interesting because demand for the services they provide is growing rapidly. There is no foreign competition and the regulatory problems keep the ease of entry low, further reducing competition.

4. One strategy for these stocks is to buy them during periods when earnings growth is slower due to regulatory delays. Earnings tend to leap ahead after approval and start-ups. However, delays can be much longer than expected due to their political nature.

5. Soft-underbelly stocks capitalize on one of our unfortunately fastest growing trends, the growth of crime and human frailty. There are not many public companies to allow investors to participate. However, I expect more to emerge during the decade; investors should watch for them. Privately managed but publicly traded prisons may become a trend.

6. Cookie-cutter stocks are numerous, frequently fast growing, and excellent investments. More importantly, they require no specialized knowledge on the part of a lay investor.

7. To make money in cookie-cutter stocks, an investor should like the concept and investigate how fast the stores are being rolled out. Generally, the faster the better; however, overly fast growth

can hurt a company in many ways. Check out management thoroughly. If the company is young, make sure the management is experienced. It is easy to lose control of these businesses.

8. "Same-store sales increases" is the growth in sales of stores open at the same time the year before. This is a key number for evaluating a cookie-cutter company. If this number is negative, the company is like a shark, it will die if it stops moving forward. If it is high, this is a very good sign (usually anything over 10 percent is high, depending on what the chain is selling). However, if same-store sales gains are too high, this may be unsustainable.

9. There are many cookie-cutters but they are mostly found in retailing and restaurants. An investor should know how profitable a single unit is relative to its peers. An investor should also know how much investment is required to open one store. From this he can calculate the per-store return on assets (pretax store profit divided by assets per store). This rate will determine, ultimately, how fast the chain can grow because money has to be raised to keep the chain growing. If the return is high, it means the concept is good and growth can be sustained. Blockbuster, a very fast-growing chain has a store rate of return of 55 percent on invested assets.

10. Some chains grow by franchising their concept. In this format, the individual investor/operators own some of or all of their own stores and the company may get an up-front fee for use of the name and an override of some kind. These chains can grow extremely fast. However, an investor should beware because what the parent is reporting as earnings may be franchise fees. This stream can end abruptly when the chain stops growing. Also a franchise system is inherently less stable and less well managed. If the company franchises excessively (more than 50 percent of new units) the multiple will be lower.

CHAPTER 18

RAGING BULL: WHY THE DOW WILL TOP 6000 BY THE LATE 90s

If you ask the average person whether the stock market goes up during periods of rising or falling corporate profits, he will probably tell you that the stock market will only go up during periods of strong economic activity, when corporate profits are robust. This common misconception is probably shared by most investors. As a result, small investors shake their heads during periods when the economy is in a recession and the market is rising rapidly, like the first quarter of 1991.

Some of the best stock market gains have been made during periods when the economy has been in a state of decline. January 1975 was an example; the second half of 1982 was another. Perhaps the most extended, however, was the period beginning in the fourth quarter of 1955 and lasting until 1962. This was a period when the market, as measured by the Dow Jones Industrial Average, increased consistently. It began in late 1955 at 488.40 and ended at 734.91, an increase of 50 percent by December 1961. Interestingly, it was a period during which corporate profits were declining. In fact, corporate profits peaked in the fourth quarter of 1955 and did not see the same level again until 1962. The trough in corporate profits was in 1957/58.

. The explanation for this paradox is simple: Every once in a while a decade offers such an exciting combination of ingredients that it leads to substantial stock market profits; the 60s was such a decade and the stock market of the 50s anticipated it. The 90s will also be such a decade. In the late 50s, a host of new consumer products were visible just over the horizon. These included color TV and jet travel, not to mention one of the most useful consumer products of the postwar period, air-conditioning. There was a certain excitement about the coming 60s in the industrial sector, too; the exploration of space (and its potential, even though Russia had beaten us with Sputnik) and the development of the computer were two factors which held a great deal of promise for growth in the future.

It was also in the late 50s that the idea of active money management became ascendant among managers of public (mutual) funds. The concept that more profits could be made by moving money around rapidly—capitalizing on changes within the market—than using a buy-and-hold strategy, began to change the nature of the market itself in the late 50s and early 60s. Growth stocks became the preferred investments for active managers, because they represented the future.

The 90s also have a sense of excitement about them which could lead to much higher valuations in the stock market. This will occur despite the fact that overall corporate profit growth may be sluggish. There are seven basic factors which we believe will be extremely important to the stock market in the decade of the 90s. They are as follows:

1. The end of the Cold War and the renewed sense of American self-confidence following the war with Iraq,
2. A high level of employment (on average),
3. Modest inflation,
4. Normal real interest rates (2–3 percent above the inflation rate),
5. Rapidly expanding exports,
6. The eventual elimination of the federal deficit, favoring American industry,
7. Rapid technological change.

Obviously it is extremely difficult to forecast rates of growth in an economy for an entire decade; most economists cannot manage it from quarter to quarter. It is only possible to give the outlines of what the economy will look like. Change occurs so fast in this society that five years ago one could have wagered a million to one against the Berlin Wall falling and Bloomingdale's and Drexel Burnham going bankrupt all in the same year and have no takers. Economic events always have their way of surprising despite the fact that there is a significant amount of inertia built into the American economy. In 1985, a war with Iran might have been considered probable, a war with Iraq absurd.

Potential for Era of Peace

Perhaps the most important characteristic of the 90s will be the potential for peace in the world, even including the Gulf region. This does not mean that the world will be without brush fire wars. Every decade since the end of World War II has had a war in which the United States has been involved, with the exception of 1980. The 50s had the Korean War, the 60s and 70s the war in Vietnam. This decade had the war with Iraq. However, since the end of World War II, two competing ideologies have battled for the hearts and minds of the world. It's hard to grasp the fact that capitalism has finally won. Even our old adversary of the Soviet Union is being forced, as though swept by a strong current, into economic reforms which more closely resemble capitalism. It is entirely likely, therefore, that with the conclusion of the Gulf War the decade of the 90s will be one in which the Western world will feel a sense of peace and security unmatched in any previous decade.

One of the great contributions of President Reagan's two terms in office was that there was no major war during his administration. It is impossible to think of any two-term president who had peace during all eight of his years in office as well as a generally expanding economy and a contracting level of inflation. Now, with the collapse of the Iron Curtain, the reunification of the Germanies, free elections being held in formerly communist countries, and the Soviet Union coming closer to a free market economy, our system of government and economic values will hold sway to a greater extent in the world. This will be very bullish for the stock market.

One of the positive attributes of the late 50s and early 60s was that the United States was so dominant in world affairs. However, the national feeling of near-omnipotence was greatly dissipated by the war in Vietnam. The feeling has returned to a large extent due to our amazing victory against Iraq. The end of the Cold War adds greatly to the security of the world. Our response to Iraq would have been more difficult if the Soviet Union had opposed us.

A Stable Economy Appearing

The second economic factor that will shape the 90s is record employment. Obviously the rate of unemployment will fluctuate during the course of the decade. Nevertheless, on balance, the United States should have a low level of unemployment. The reason for this is fairly simple: there are approximately 240 million people in the United States (recorded by the census of 1988). Over the next 10 years the country is expected to grow to about 260 million people. Of those, approximately 12 million will be in the 45 to 54-year-old-age bracket. This bulge in population is generally known as the war "baby boom."

186 Part 2 Growth Areas of the 90s

As the war babies have pushed their way through each age bracket, different effects have occurred within the country, both politically and economically. During the decade of the 80s, the war babies were forming families. They also included a large number of people who were seeking employment, and a great many new jobs had to be created to accommodate them. Now, as the war babies approach middle age (I like to think of 50 as middle age even though the average person certainly does not live to be 100), the economic priorities of this vast aggregation of people will be quite different. The people in the 45–50 age bracket have as their main priority, investment, not consumption; most of the baby boomers have already bought houses and had families. Major consumption items such as furniture, cars, stereos, and so forth have already been acquired. The surge in buying of luxury goods that occurred in the 1980s probably will subside; replacing it will be an increased level of savings. As the generation matures, they will be looking toward retirement within 15 to 20 years; this retirement will probably not be manageable with social security and pension funds alone. Consequently, the baby boomers will be needing to supplement their income in retirement. The United States has recently had a savings rate far lower than that of its trading partners. This has been blamed for a variety of ills including the large foreign investment in our government debt, equity markets, and real estate. Also, it has been blamed for the inadequate rejuvenation of our industrial capacity and the uncompetitive nature of our industries.

This logic is not entirely correct. Foreigners, especially the Japanese, invest in our securities because they are forced to buy either American products, which seem to be restricted deliberately by trade policy, or American financial assets. As the dollar is a reserve currency, it is incumbent upon them to find some use for the dollars they accumulate by selling us cars, televisions, etc. The most logical use for their excess dollars, therefore, becomes investment in the United States. This is not totally an explicit function of our low level of investment.

The boom in the Japanese exports to the United States has not been all bad. It has helped immeasurably in keeping down our cost of living, a fact which is frequently not recognized by those bashing Japan (and Korea, Taiwan, etc.). However, as the population matures, as it certainly will in the 90s, the overall desire to consume will diminish and the desire to invest will increase. This will have a tendency of tilting the balance away from the importation of products to a competition with foreigners for our financial assets.

One of the most important factors about our increasing level of investment and savings will be its effect on the stock market. The fastest way to provide for retirement is to compound money at a high rate and preferably tax free. Tax deferral can be accomplished by buying annuities (a form of tax-deferred mutual fund), and there is no question that one of the fastest ways to compound money in a major category of financial assets is the stock market. Thus the rising level of savings/investment and the dropping level of consumption will mean increased demand for common stocks on the part of the individual investor. This will cause a large and rapid expansion of mutual fund assets and, more importantly, a rapid increase in the valuation of common stocks. This in turn will spawn another effect; as prices of common stocks rise, the ability of companies to finance with equity rather than debt will increase. As a consequence, the economy will go through a re-equitization, which is the reduction in the amount of private debt outstanding and an increase in the amount of equity capital.

Whereas the 80s saw a net withdrawal of money from the stock market, I believe the 90s will see net increases in the dollar amount of common stock, as companies rebalance their balance sheets in favor of equity, taking advantage of rising prices. This should have a salutary effect on the American economy. It will provide capital for newer, more rapidly growing, businesses and accelerate the refurbishment of antiquated plant, making us a more vital world competitor.

Inflation under Control

The next important factor for the stock market in the 90s will be a comparatively low inflation rate. Contrary to popular wisdom, inflation is not created by the supply and demand for commodities. Evidence of this came after the breakdown of the Bretton Woods monetary agreement in 1971. At that time, all commodities rose dramatically in price, and they rose in lockstep fashion. All commodity prices rose, even including those which were in abundant supply and for which demand was perceptibly weak.

We believe that inflation is a psychological, or attitudinally driven phenomenon. When conditions lead people to believe that inflation is increasing, they tend to invest in hard assets and hedge themselves against increasing commodity prices. This in turn creates its own inflation. A short anecdote will explain how this works:

I once met the Chief Financial Officer of the Argentinian subsidiary of an American auto company. At the time that he was so employed, Argentina was going through one of its frequent bouts of hyper-inflation. The local currency was devaluing so rapidly that even a day of holding the currency meant significantly reduced purchasing power. Thus, when local currency receipts were collected on Friday afternoon, there was a mad scramble to convert the currency into *any* hard asset. He told me that one Friday he was reduced to buying a thousand large industrial pallets, for which he had no use and did not know how to dispose of; they were simply the only hard assets available. Similarly, during periods of elevated inflation in our country, people tend to attach themselves to hard assets.

These hard assets are not necessarily industrial raw materials or Impressionist paintings; the American housewife has a mental computer that continuously weighs the rate of increase in cost of living (inflation) against the economic return on her savings account. If she believes that the price of refrigerators is increasing 15 percent a year, she will withdraw money from a 10 percent savings account to buy a refrigerator, in order to beat the price increase. Conversely, should inflation subside, money that the housewife might spend on hard assets will instead be saved for the future, probably in a mutual fund.

This kind of transaction is the invisible link between the world of financial assets and the world of real assets. In the 90s the policy put into effect by the Federal Reserve Board in 1979 will continue to have a dampening effect on inflation. This policy emphasizes a rapid reaction to inflation by the aggressive tightening of money. As long as people believe the Fed will control inflation then inflationary psychology will be dampened. More importantly, the tendency of the older population to save rather than spend will likewise keep inflation down. We believe moreover, that the economy will be growing at a positive but slower rate during the decade of the 90s, and as a consequence, inflation will be contained not from the absence of demand, but because of the perception that the price of goods will be repetitively reduced (sales) or will not be growing at a rapid rate.

Positive Real Interest Rates

A corollary to the low inflation thesis is that in the 1990s there will be a period of consistently positive real interest rates. Real interest rates—defined as the 10-year government bond yield less the CPI—have fluctuated substantially during the past 20 years (see Figure 18–1). They first became negative in July 1973 when the market failed to appreciate the severity and the potential duration of the inflationary cycle. At its worst point, in 1974, the yield on 10-year government bonds hit 7.6 percent and the consumer price index was 12.3 percent, creating a negative real rate of interest of nearly 5 percent. By the time the market had begun to accept the endemic rate of inflation and began demanding very much higher interest rates, it was 1981 and inflation was already in a process of declining due to the new Fed policy. From 1982 through 1989 the CPI never exceeded 5 percent. However, by 1984 the real rate of interest was exceptionally high as people refused to accept the fact that inflation had largely abated.

Normally the real rate of interest is about 2–3 percent and the rate remains slightly above that at present. We believe that this year should see the completion of the cycle and rates will once again return to the 2–3 percent level. They will remain there for much of the 90s. A positive but not excessive rate of return will have several effects. First, it will keep the dollar from becoming too weak; second, it will tend to keep a lid on inflation; third, it will continue to encourage the financing of government debt on the part of foreign investors. On the other hand, it will not be a high enough rate so that bonds will be overly competitive with stocks.

Expanding American Exports

The next important factor that will influence the market is that American exports should be expanding rapidly in the 90s. There are several reasons why this is so. First of all, American industry is substantially more competitive than at any time in its recent past. Intense competition from the Japanese has brought rationalization of factories, closing down of obsolete plants, scrapping of old equipment and investing in new methods of manufacturing. More importantly, our exports will be increasingly high-tech in nature in the 90s. Here the law of comparative advantage will very much work to our favor. I believe that in the 90s, the pace of technology will accelerate. This acceleration will see America reclaiming from the Japanese part of its lost market share in electronics and other types of goods.

The advantage will go to the United States because our greater capacity for design and innovation will replace the Japanese advantage in mass manufacturing. Products will evolve progressively more rapidly and design flexibility, rather than efficient production lines, will determine the

FIGURE 18–1
Real Interest Rates (10-year government bond yield less CPI)

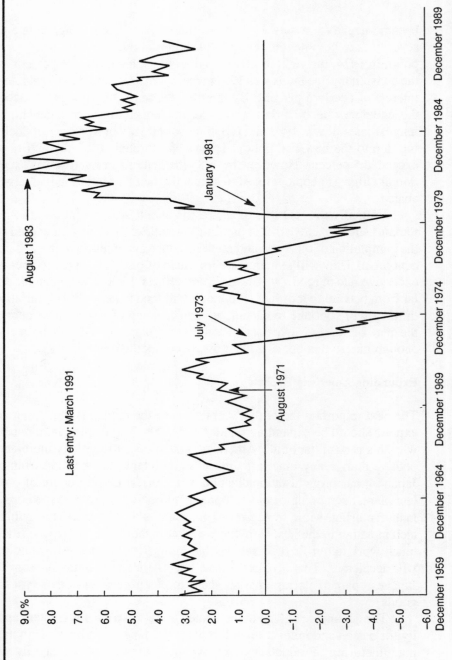

FIGURE 18–1 (concluded)
Real Interest Rates (10-year government bond yield less CPI)

Last Entry: March 1991

	1961	1962	1963	1964	1965	1966	1967	1968	1969	1970	1971	1972	1973	1974	1975
10-year govt. bonds	3.9%	4.0%	4.0%	4.2%	4.3%	4.9%	5.1%	5.7%	6.7%	7.4%	6.2%	6.2%	6.8%	7.6%	8.0%
CPI	0.7	1.3	1.6	1.0	1.9	3.5	3.0	4.7	6.2	5.6	3.3	3.4	8.7	12.3	6.9

	1976	1977	1978	1979	1980	1981	1982	1983	1984	1985	1986	1987	1988	1989	1990
10-year govt. bonds	7.6%	7.4%	8.4%	9.4%	11.5%	13.9%	13.0%	11.1%	12.4%	10.7%	7.7%	8.4%	8.9%	8.5%	8.6%
CPI	4.9	6.7	9.0	13.3	12.5	8.9	3.8	3.8	3.9	3.8	1.1	4.4	4.4	4.6	6.1

Source: Fred Alger Management, Inc.

nature of the market. Rapidly expanding exports combined with real rates of interest should help the dollar remain stable in the international market place. This will in turn help to reduce our inflation. At the same time, the dollar will also be enhanced by the comparative lack of consumption due to the aging of the population. A good portion of our merchandise trade deficit relates to the importation of consumer items, in some cases made by American companies overseas.

It is highly significant that by the mid-90s a variety of new markets should be opening up to American products. The availability of the formerly communist world as a market for American consumer products as well as high technology industrial products, will create a boom for American exports. This is a market that can be served by the United States from both a cultural and geographical perspective; because of America's strong base of trading with Western Europe, it is logical that a great deal of this market can be captured for the United States. Additionally, the opening up of Eastern Europe will greatly strengthen some of our vital trade partners in Western Europe, such as Germany and France. It will take at least five years to achieve a state of critical mass in exporting to Eastern European countries or to the larger, presently socialist countries such as the Soviet Union or China. During that time there will be many attempts and a very uneven flow of business. The opening of the markets will be important for the stock market. The market is governed by psychology, and the American market has been suffering from depression due to feelings of inferiority versus the Japanese. This will change as our trade balance improves.

Eliminating the Federal Deficit

Another factor that should be extraordinarily bullish for the 1990s is that by the year 2000, if present trends continue in place, the buildup in the Social Security trust fund will be sufficient to eliminate the federal budget deficit (see Table 18–1). Twenty years later, the Social Security trust fund will entirely eliminate all government debt held in private hands. There has been a great deal written recently about whether to take the social security trust fund entirely off the balance sheet. The elimination of the federal deficit will occur much later if Social Security is deconsolidated. Last year, the passage of the Omnibus Reconciliation Act (November 1990) removed the financial operations of the trust funds from calculation of the federal budget deficit targets for purposes of the

Gramm-Rudman-Hollings Act. However, the fact is that, at present, the social security trust fund *must buy* American government bonds. Consequently, the surplus that will build up within it (whether or not it is deconsolidated) will be used to absorb all the debt that is created as a by-product of the deficit in the other parts of the government.

The main problem with having a deficit is the need to rely on outside investors to finance it. This results in increasing volatility of markets and consequently, higher interest rates. This concern will be eliminated. The American taxpayer, who is taxed to provide for the social security system, will be filling the coffers of the trust fund, and those funds will be used to buy the bonds issued by the rest of the American government.

By the year 2020, if the Social Security Administration's own projections are accurate, all private debt whether owned by an American person, an institution, or a Japanese entity, will be bought by the Social Security trust fund. There will be no government debt held in private hands at that point.

In theory, this means that the yield on government bonds will, effectively, become zero as all bonds are retired. This is hard to imagine without Congress changing the rules in some way so as to tap this vast resource, but it is nevertheless theoretically possible.

Even now there is talk of reducing the FICA tax. This will probably not be approved however. Most important is the fact that by the end of this decade, the deficit will be so reduced as to cause substantial downward pressure on interest rates. This will cause an increase in common stock valuations, as well as provide a comparably cheaper form of debt financing for companies who are attempting to grow in the late 90s. Table 18–2 illustrates the impact of the Social Security trust fund on the national debt.

More Technological Change Ahead

Lastly, the pace of technology continues to accelerate. The great success of our weapons in the war with Iraq have encouraged us all in our faith in American technology. In this book some of the new and exciting technologies have been covered. Their emergence will be a stimulating factor in the stock market, as it was in the late 50s, when investors looked at the 60s.

In summary, the nineties will be a decade of slower but reasonably persistent growth with a much higher savings rate than in the recent past. It will be a stable decade, with low inflation and low but real interest rates

TABLE 18–1

Projected Social Security Trust Fund Assets and the Federal Budget (on a calendar-year basis)

	On-Budget Deficit/Surplus, including Interest Expense	As a % of GNP	Social Security Deficit/Surplus	Unified Budget Deficit/Surplus	Interest Rate Percent	Federal Debt at Year-end Total	Net of On-Budget Govt. Holdings	Net of Social Security Holdings	Social Security Assets at Year-end
1985	($224.6)	−5.6%	$ 9.0	($215.6)	10.8%	$1,950.3	$1,643.6	$1,601.4	$ 42.2
1986	(226.3)	−5.3	4.7	(221.6)	8.0	2,218.9	1,861.2	1,814.7	46.9
1987	(170.9)	−3.8	21.9	(148.9)	8.4	2,435.2	2,017.2	1,956.8	68.8
1988	(199.1)	−4.1	41.0	(158.1)	8.8	2,707.3	2,213.2	2,103.2	109.8
1989	(207.6)	−4.0	53.2	(154.4)	8.7	2,975.5	2,411.9	2,248.7	163.0
1990	(296.9)	−5.4	62.7	(234.1)	8.3	3,397.3	2,816.3	2,498.1	225.7
1991	(382.1)	−6.7	65.3	(316.8)	8.0	3,779.4	3,144.4	2,853.4	291.0
1992	(353.7)	−5.8	72.6	(281.1)	7.7	4,133.1	3,436.1	3,072.5	363.6
1993	(299.7)	−4.6	79.9	(219.8)	7.6	4,432.8	3,364.1	2,920.6	443.5
1994	(185.1)	−2.7	91.1	($94.0)	7.3	4,617.9	3,773.9	3,239.3	534.6
1995	(175.4)	−2.4	101.9	($73.5)	6.9	4,793.3	3,872.3	3,235.8	636.5
1996	(171.0)	−2.2	114.8	($56.2)	6.5	4,964.3	3,969.3	3,218.0	751.3
1997	(182.7)	−2.2	127.2	($55.5)	6.4	5,147.0	4,152.0	3,273.5	878.5
1998	(175.2)	−2.0	140.4	($34.8)	6.3	5,322.3	4,327.3	3,308.4	1,018.9
1999	(161.3)	−1.7	154.2	($7.1)	6.1	5,483.6	4,488.6	3,315.5	1,173.1
2000	(149.9)	−1.5	166.8	$16.9	6.0	5,633.5	4,638.5	3,298.6	1,339.9
2001	(139.9)	−1.3	177.5	$37.6	6.0	5,773.4	4,778.4	3,261.0	1,517.4
2002	(127.6)	−1.1	187.5	$59.9	6.0	5,901.0	4,906.0	3,201.1	1,704.9
2003	(112.7)	−1.0	217.5	$104.8	6.0	6,013.7	5,018.7	3,096.3	1,922.4
2004	(94.8)	−0.8	247.5	$152.7	6.0	6,108.5	5,113.5	2,943.6	2,169.9
2005	(73.7)	−0.6	292.7	$219.0	6.0	6,182.2	5,187.2	2,724.6	2,462.6
2006	(49.3)	−0.3	295.7	$246.4	6.0	6,231.6	5,236.6	2,478.3	2,758.3
2007	(21.1)	−0.1	305.9	$284.8	6.0	6,252.7	5,257.7	2,193.5	3,064.2

TABLE 18–1 (concluded)
Projected Social Security Trust Fund Assets and the Federal Budget (on a calendar-year basis)

	On-Budget Deficit/ Surplus, including Interest Expense	As a % of GNP	Social Security Deficit/ Surplus	Unified Budget Deficit/ Surplus	Interest Rate Percent	Federal Debt at Year-end			Social Security Assets at Year-end
						Total	Net of On-Budget Govt. Holdings	Net of Social Security Holdings	
2008	$ 11.5	0.1	325.9	$337.4	6.0	$6,241.1	$5,246.1	$1,856.0	$3,390.1
2009	49.0	0.3	345.9	$394.9	6.0	6,192.1	5,197.1	1,461.1	3,736.0
2010	91.7	0.5	356.1	$447.8	6.0	6,100.4	5,105.4	1,013.3	4,092.1
2011	137.5	0.7	367.8	$505.3	6.0	5,962.9	4,967.9	508.0	4,459.9
2012	189.1	1.0	378.0	$567.1	6.0	5,773.8	4,778.8	(59.1)	4,837.9
2013	247.1	1.2	398.0	$645.1	6.0	5,526.7	4,531.7	(704.2)	5,235.9
2014	312.1	1.4	418.0	$730.1	6.0	5,214.6	4,219.6	(1,434.3)	5,653.9
2015	384.8	1.6	428.4	$813.2	6.0	4,829.7	3,834.7	(2,247.6)	6,082.3
2016	464.9	1.9	438.3	$903.2	6.0	4,364.8	3,369.8	(3,150.8)	6,520.6
2017	553.9	2.1	418.7	$972.6	6.0	3,810.9	2,815.9	(4,123.4)	6,939.3
2018	651.5	2.4	378.7	$1,030.2	6.0	3,159.3	2,164.3	(5,153.7)	7,318.0
2019	759.6	2.6	338.7	$1,098.3	6.0	2,399.8	1,404.8	(6,251.9)	7,656.7
2020	878.9	2.9	318.9	$1,197.8	6.0	1,520.9	525.9	(7,449.7)	7,975.6

1. Social security outlays in 1987 included the payment of January 1988 benefits, thereby reducing the 1987 surplus.
2. Federal debt represents all Treasury securities. Federal debt net of government holdings, including social security investments, represents total debt in the hands of the public, including the Federal Reserve.
3. The increase in social security assets in 1986 was less than the surplus in that year since a portion of the surplus was used to repay the loan owed to the Hospital Insurance Trust Fund.

Source: Fred Alger Management, January 1991.

TABLE 18–2

Projected Social Security Trust Fund Assets and the Federal Budget (on a calendar-year basis)

	Nominal GNP, Using II-B		On-Budget Revenues			On-Budget Outlays, Excluding Interest			Operating Deficit/Surplus Ex. Interest		Interest Expense		
		Year/Year		As a % of GNP	Year/Year		As a % of GNP	Year/Year	As a % of GNP		Gross	Net On-Budget Interest	Net Interest
1985	$4,014.9		$556.5	13.9%		$644.1	16.0%		–2.2%	($87.6)	$180.4	$137.0	$132.6
1986	4,231.6	5.4%	577.3	13.6	3.7%	664.1	15.7	3.1%	–2.1	(86.8)	191.8	139.5	134.8
1987	4,515.6	6.7	652.3	14.4	13.0	675.1	14.9	1.7	–0.5	(22.8)	201.0	148.1	142.0
1988	4,873.7	7.9	680.5	14.0	4.3	716.1	14.7	6.1	–0.7	(35.5)	221.3	163.5	154.4
1989	5,200.8	6.7	731.0	14.1	7.4	750.9	14.4	4.9	–0.4	(20.0)	250.3	187.6	173.9
1990	5,463.0	5.0	767.7	14.1	5.0	861.0	15.8	14.7	–1.7	(93.3)	273.9	203.6	185.1
1991	5,670.8	3.8	796.9	14.1	3.8	974.6	17.2	13.2	–3.1	(177.8)	271.8	204.3	199.8
1992	6,050.7	6.7	850.2	14.1	6.7	987.9	16.3	1.4	–2.3	(137.6)	291.0	216.1	219.7
1993	6,456.1	6.7	907.2	14.1	6.7	975.8	15.1	–1.2	–1.1	(68.6)	314.1	231.1	233.5
1994	6,869.3	6.4	965.3	14.1	6.4	934.7	13.6	–4.2	0.4	30.5	323.6	215.6	213.2
1995	7,309.0	6.4	1,027.1	14.1	6.4	970.0	13.3	3.8	0.8	57.0	318.6	232.4	223.5
1996	7,776.7	6.4	1,092.8	14.1	6.4	1,035.1	13.3	6.7	0.7	57.7	311.6	228.7	210.3
1997	8,274.5	6.4	1,162.7	14.1	6.4	1,091.4	13.2	5.4	0.9	71.3	317.7	254.0	206.0
1998	8,804.0	6.4	1,237.1	14.1	6.4	1,150.8	13.1	5.4	1.0	86.3	324.3	261.6	206.2
1999	9,358.7	6.3	1,315.1	14.1	6.3	1,212.4	13.0	5.4	1.1	102.7	324.7	264.0	201.8
2000	9,910.8	5.9	1,392.7	14.1	5.9	1,273.2	12.8	5.0	1.2	119.4	329.0	269.3	198.9
2001	10,515.4	6.1	1,477.6	14.1	6.1	1,339.2	12.7	5.2	1.3	138.4	338.0	278.3	197.9
2002	11,156.8	6.1	1,567.8	14.1	6.1	1,408.7	12.6	5.2	1.4	159.1	346.4	286.7	195.7
2003	11,837.4	6.1	1,663.4	14.1	6.1	1,481.7	12.5	5.2	1.5	181.7	354.1	294.4	192.1
2004	12,559.5	6.1	1,764.9	14.1	6.1	1,558.6	12.4	5.2	1.6	206.3	360.8	301.1	185.8
2005	13,325.6	6.1	1,872.5	14.1	6.1	1,639.4	12.3	5.2	1.7	233.1	366.5	306.8	176.6
2006	14,125.1	6.0	1,984.9	14.1	6.0	1,723.0	12.2	5.1	1.9	261.9	370.9	311.2	163.5
2007	14,972.7	6.0	2,104.0	14.1	6.0	1,810.8	12.1	5.1	2.0	293.1	373.9	314.2	148.7
2008	15,871.0	6.0	2,230.2	14.1	6.0	1,903.2	12.0	5.1	2.1	327.0	375.2	315.5	131.6
2009	16,823.3	6.0	2,364.0	14.1	6.0	2,000.3	11.9	5.1	2.2	363.7	374.5	314.8	111.4
2010	17,832.7	6.0	2,505.8	14.1	6.0	2,102.3	11.8	5.1	2.3	403.6	371.5	311.8	87.7
2011	18,831.3	5.6	2,646.2	14.1	5.6	2,202.3	11.7	4.8	2.4	443.8	366.0	306.3	60.8

TABLE 18–2 (concluded)
Projected Social Security Trust Fund Assets and the Federal Budget (on a calendar-year basis)

	Nominal GNP, Using II-B		On-Budget Revenues			On-Budget Outlays, Excluding Interest			Operating Deficit/Surplus Ex. Interest		Interest Expense		
		Year/ Year		As a % of GNP	Year/ Year		As a % of GNP	Year/ Year		As a % of GNP	Gross	Net On-Budget Interest	Net Interest
2012	19,885.9	5.6	2,794.4	14.1	5.6	2,307.2	11.6	4.8	487.2	2.4	357.8	298.1	30.5
2013	20,999.5	5.6	2,950.8	14.1	5.6	2,417.0	11.5	4.8	533.8	2.5	346.4	286.7	(3.5)
2014	22,175.4	5.6	3,116.1	14.1	5.6	2,532.0	11.4	4.8	584.0	2.6	331.6	271.9	(42.3)
2015	23,417.3	5.6	3,290.6	14.1	5.6	2,652.6	11.3	4.8	638.0	2.7	312.9	253.2	(86.1)
2016	24,705.2	5.5	3,471.6	14.1	5.5	2,776.6	11.2	4.7	695.0	2.8	289.8	230.1	(134.9)
2017	26,064.0	5.5	3,662.5	14.1	5.5	2,906.4	11.2	4.7	756.1	2.9	261.9	202.2	(189.0)
2018	27,471.5	5.4	3,860.3	14.1	5.4	3,039.8	11.1	4.6	820.5	3.0	228.7	169.0	(247.4)
2019	28,954.9	5.4	4,068.7	14.1	5.4	3,179.3	11.0	4.6	889.4	3.1	189.6	129.9	(309.2)
2020	30,518.5	5.4	4,288.4	14.1	5.4	3,325.2	10.9	4.6	963.2	3.2	144.0	84.3	(375.1)

1. Long-range forecasts (1997–2020) for social security assets, nominal GNP, and interest rate assumptions are based on Social Security Administration projections, as published in the 1989 annual report.

2. On-budget federal revenues are assumed to grow at the same rate as nominal GNP.

3. Long-range (1997–2020) on-budget federal outlays, excluding interest expense, are assumed to grow at 85 percent of nominal GNP's growth rate, in line with the latest 5-year trend. Short-term projections (1991–96) are based on Office of Management and Budget forecasts.

4. The operating deficit represents the difference between revenues and outlays, excluding interest expense.

5. Interest expense is derived by multiplying the interest rate by the appropriate debt figure. Gross interest expense represents total interest on all federal debt. Net on-budget includes all on-budget offsetting interest receipts. Net interest includes interest paid to the Social Security trust fund (OASDI).

Source: Fred Alger Management, January 1991.

197

until the end of the decade when the elimination of the federal deficit could force interest rates even lower. Through most of the decade, the dollar should be stable and exports should be strong especially in mid-decade and beyond, when Eastern Europe and the Soviet Union develop sufficiently to open up new markets for American products. It will be a decade characterized by investment and a feeling of peace and prosperity. In such an environment, multiples in the stock market will expand to high levels, permitting the Dow Jones Industrial Average to exceed 6000 (Dow earnings 375×16 P/E $= 6000$) by the late 90s. Will there be problems? Of course. There is never a period without problems. But it will be a great period for growth stock investing!

GLOSSARY OF FINANCIAL TERMS

active management   An investing style by which the manager tries to do better than one or all of the averages.

analyst   A person who evaluates the prospects for groups of stocks.

annual report   This document is sent to the shareholders of public companies after each fiscal year. It contains the financial statements as well as management's comments on the year and often a lot of pretty pictures.

assets   What the company owns.

audit   Accountants calculate the company's results; certified public accountant must do this formally and attest to the accuracy of the numbers at each year end for all publicly traded corporations. This is called an audit and the accounting firm is called the auditor.

balance sheet   Statement issued at the end of an accounting period showing the assets, liabilities and equity at the close of business on the last day of the period.

board of directors   Group of individuals elected by shareholders to represent their interests. The "board" hires the management that may or may not be some or all of the same people.

book value   Net worth per share. To calculate: total shareholders equity divided by number of shares outstanding.

cash flow   Generally, it means net income plus depreciation. It can have other similar definitions.

common stock   Certificates issued in the form of shares that all together represent the ownership of a corporation.

company   An organization involved in a commercial enterprise.

corporation   A company that is incorporated, conferring upon it its own legal status.

cost of goods sold   The expense involved in the direct production of the product the company sells.

current assets   Assets expected to be gone in less than a year.

current liabilities   Liabilities expected to be satisfied in less than one year.

depreciation   An expense that is artificially created to reflect the deterioration of assets. While it reduces the profit it doesn't require any cash expenditure.

dividends   Money the board of directors elect to pay out of earnings to share-holders. It is usually, but not always, a fraction of the earnings of the company.

earnings growth   How much earnings per share have increased over the comparable period the year before.

earnings per share (P/E)   Net income divided by number of shares outstanding after deduction of preferred dividends, if any.

equity   Ownership. That which is owned by the common shareholders. Also called shareholders' equity or net worth, it represents assets minus liabilities.

fiscal quarter   A fiscal year is made up of four quarters, usually of three months each (they are not always exactly the same length). The company reports its results each quarter and for the year as a whole. Only the year's results must be audited.

fiscal year   The company's accounting year. A company can pick any month it wants its year to end on but December (called a calendar year) is the over-whelming favorite, followed by June, and in the case of retailers, January.

fundamental analysis   Determining the prospects for a stock by analysing the business prospects of the company.

gross profit   Sales less cost of goods sold.

growth fund   A fund which specializes in investing in growth stocks.

growth stocks   Companies whose earnings per share can be expected to grow significantly faster than the economy.

income statement   Also called profit and loss statement (P&L). Mathematical history of an accounting period, showing revenues, expenses, and profits (or losses).

interest expense   Cost of borrowing money.

large cap. stocks   Above the limit of small cap (see "small cap. stocks")

liabilities   What the company owes. Technically, equity is a liability because it is what a company owes to its shareholders.

listed stock   Stock traded on an exchange such as the New York Stock Exchange.

long-term debt   Debt due after one year.

market value   Also called market capitalization. Price of the stock times the total number of shares outstanding. The theoretical total value of the company.

buying on margin   Borrowing money from a broker to buy stocks.

mutual fund   A fund that can be invested in by an individual but which is managed by a professional portfolio manager, thus providing professional management and diversification for a fee.

net income   Also "net profit" or "net earnings" or "earnings." Pre-tax profit minus federal income and state income taxes.

new issue   A company selling its shares to the public for the very first time. A primary issue.

operating expenses   Expenses of operations; sometimes includes depreciation and interest.

passive management   A style where the manager tries to duplicate one of the averages, usually the S&P 500.

payout ratio   Dividends per share divided by earnings per share.

preliminary prospectus   Also called a "red herring," it is issued before primary or secondary distribution and has a wealth of data about the company, but not the price of the offering.

profit margin   Can be net margin or pre-tax. It is calculated by taking earnings and dividing them by sales.

portfolio manager   A person who invests money for another party in the stock market by buying a group of stocks for him.

pre-tax profit   Profit after expenses are deducted but before taxes are.

prospectus   A document distributed immediately after a primary or secondary offering, includes final terms of offer such as price and commissions.

publicly traded   A corporation whose shares are in whole or in part owned by the general public and traded.

revenues   Dollars received for shipping merchandise, performing a service, or in some other way, such as receiving interest from owning bonds.

sales   Revenues from selling things. A subset of revenues.

secondary   A large-scale, registered offering of stock by a company already public. It can be new stock, sold by the corporation or a bulk sale by a group of selling shareholders.

sector fund   A mutual fund that only buys stocks of one or several similar industries.

securities & exchange commission "SEC" Regulates securities and trading under federal law.

S.G.&A. Selling, General, and Administrative expenses involved with general corporate activities such as advertising.

shares Unit of common stock. Basically a corporation can have as many shares issued and outstanding as it wishes but all together they constitute 100 percent ownership.

small cap. stocks Stocks whose market values are smaller. Precise definitions vary. We consider it below $1 billion.

stockbroker A professional through whom stocks are bought or sold.

symbol Used to identify a stock for purposes of trading. Listed stocks generally have a three-letter symbol, NASDAQ stocks have a four-letter symbol.

technical analysis Determining the prospects for a stock or the whole market by analysing trading patterns as opposed to fundamental analysis.

10-K A document containing the financial statements (but no pretty pictures) filed with the SEC each year.

traded on NASDAQ Shares traded among a vast network of dealers who make markets electronically. NASDAQ stocks usually have a four-letter symbol.

unit volume growth The percentage increase in the number of units the company sold compared to the same period the year before. This assumes the units are roughly comparable in nature.

value stocks Companies with strong balance sheets and/or hidden assets, but not necessarily much earnings growth.

volume Amount of shares traded (usually per day). NASDAQ volume is double-counted because they consider the buy and the sell to be two transactions.

working capital Current assets minus current liabilities.

yield Dividends per share divided by price of the stock.

INDEX